Ask the Masters!

Ask the masters!

Making the Most of Your Scrapbook Supplies

From the Memory Makers Masters

Memory Makers Books
Cincinnati, Ohio
www.memorymakersmagazine.com
www.fwbookstore.com

Making the Most of Your Scrapbook Supplies. Copyright © 2007 by Memory Makers Books. Manufactured in China. All rights reserved. It is permissible for the purchaser to make the projects contained herein and sell them at fairs, bazaars and craft shows. No other part of this book may be reproduced in any form or by any electronic or mechanical means including information storage and retrieval systems without permission in writing from the publisher, except by a reviewer, who may quote a brief passage in review. Published by Memory Makers Books, an imprint of F+W Publications, Inc., 4700 East Galbraith Road, Cincinnati, Ohio 45236. (800) 289-0963. First edition.

11 10 09 08 07   5 4 3 2 1

Distributed in Canada by Fraser Direct
100 Armstrong Avenue
Georgetown, ON, Canada L7G 5S4
Tel: (905) 877-4411

Distributed in the U.K. and Europe by David & Charles
Brunel House, Newton Abbot, Devon, TQ12 4PU, England
Tel: (+44) 1626 323200, Fax: (+44) 1626 323319
E-mail: postmaster@davidandcharles.co.uk

Distributed in Australia by Capricorn Link
P.O. Box 704, S. Windsor, NSW 2756 Australia
Tel: (02) 4577-3555

Library of Congress Cataloging-in-Publication Data
Making the most of your scrapbook supplies.
     p. cm. -- (Ask the masters!)
  Includes index.
  ISBN-13: 978-1-59963-012-0 (alk. paper)
  ISBN-10: 1-59963-012-5 (alk. paper)
  1. Photograph albums. 2. Photographs--Conservation and restoration. 3. Scrapbooks.
TR465.M356 2007
745.593--dc22
                              2007015279

fw

F+W PUBLICATIONS, INC.
www.fwbookstore.com

Editor: Christine Doyle
Writer: Darlene D'Agnostino
Designer: Kelly O'Dell
Art Coordinator: Eileen Aber
Production Coordinator: Matt Wagner
Photographer: Tim Grondin
Stylist: Jan Nickum

If you are interested in participating in the next Memory Makers Masters contest, you can get more information at **www.memorymakersmagazine.com.** *And while you're there, check out the blogs by the current year's Masters.*

The opportunity to coordinate books in the Ask the Masters series is one of my favorite duties of the year. I contact the current class and the alumni, inquiring about availability and schedules. I make assignments, giving each participant their questions to answer. And then I wait. Wait with growing anticipation, wondering, "What kind of answers are they going to come up with for the questions this time?" And each year, I am amazed. Amazed by the talent, creativity and cleverness of this group of ladies— these Memory Makers Masters.

Who exactly makes up this group of "masters," you may ask? They are the cream of the scrapbooking crop, so to speak. Each year since 2003, Memory Makers has held a contest in search of innovative scrapbookers. Of the hundreds of entries we receive, only ten scrapbookers are selected to be that year's Memory Makers Masters.

This book that you hold in your hands includes the work of all of our 2007 Masters as well as that of many talented Masters from previous years. As you look through the layouts and projects presented here, I hope you feel that same sense of anticipation and excitement as I did, that you too are amazed and inspired and by these fabulous Masters.

Enjoy!

Christine Doyle
Executive Editor, Memory Makers Books

TABLE OF contents

16 YOUR FORGOTTEN tools

1

40 STALE supplies

2

introduction

Inside this book is scrapbooking resourcefulness. That's right. It's going to teach you how to freshen up old favorites, fondly remember tools and supplies you've forgotten and use the unused. We love our Masters for their artistic genius, but it's really their ingenuity that impresses us, figuring out how to maximize their product purchases, discovering new and unconventional ways to use old favorites and maintaining an attitude of "waste not, want not" when it comes to cleverly using supply scraps.

After you start reading this book, we hope you will begin looking at your tools and supplies in a new way, asking yourself the following questions:

✳ Exactly how many ways can I use this thing? I know (insert name of tool or supply here) has an intended purpose, but what would happen if I used it like THIS?

✳ Hello, scrap pile! What can I do with you little leftovers? How can I mix items for unexpected results?

✳ What other areas of my life could benefit from leftover creativity? The fridge? My car? Pocketbook? Work bulletin board? How can my scrapbook skills influence every part of my life for the better?

Never again should you look at your supply stash with an air of discontent. Instead, if you are out of something, you will improvise. If you purchased something, you will no doubt put it to good use. If you have gobs and gobs of something, you will figure out multiple ways in which to use it. You will have faith in yourself and your creative spirit. Courageous creative endeavors lead to unlocked potential you never realized existed.

If you strive to be like a Master, chances are, you already are. You see, the Memory Makers Masters have disorganized stashes, buy things they don't use and suffer creative block. You might be surprised to find that their signature supplies are basics. When asked to list her favorite supply, most Masters said, "paper." They also love paint and ink, which allow them to alter most anything, and chipboard, because of its versatility. Want to be masterlike? Challenge yourself to find creativity in your basic supplies, and your art will soar.

JESSIE BALDWIN

What is your favorite scrapbooking supply? Why?

Paint. With paint, you can change anything. All of a sudden a simple piece of paper takes on a whole new life. Odd-colored stickers are new again when they are all painted a single color. A blah, ordinary embellishment becomes extraordinary with a few strokes of my paintbrush. And of course, any time I use my paints, I feel like a real artist.

VALERIE BARTON

What is your favorite scrapbooking supply? Why?

I am in love with alphabet rub-ons!!! I have an endless supply, yet I buy more every time I go to a scrapbooking store. I am not technologically savvy, so I avoid computer-generated titles and journaling. Rub-ons are the easiest way for me to create interesting titles and add comments to my pages.

BROOKE BARTIMIOLI

What is your favorite scrapbooking supply? Why?

I couldn't do without ink pads, but primarily Coffee Bean by Rubber Stampede. I go crazy if every edge of my paper isn't inked. It works well with my collage-y, altered-book style. I also love the layered look, so the inky edges help add distinction.

JENNIFER BOURGEAULT

What supply do you spend the most money on?

Letter stickers! While I love creating handcut titles, I can't resist splurging on every new package of letter stickers I see. They make doing titles so quick and easy. Plus there is a variety; there is a letter sticker to fit every page theme.

CHRISTINE BROWN

What did you love about this project?

I created two layouts for this project and they ended up being two of my all-time faves. I really wasn't expecting them to be, given that I had to use "old" supplies. This project forced me to be creative in ways other than just "how can you use these cool new products." The resulting pages are both beautiful and uniquely creative.

SUSAN CYRUS

What do you buy and never use?

Patterned paper. I always buy it, but never use it. In fact, something fishy happens with it. For, whenever I actually want to use it, I can't seem to find it. On the flip side, I am the queen of white cardstock. I just can't scrapbook without it.

LISA DIXON

What supplies do you keep within arm's reach?

I have a Total-lly Cool Tote from All My Memories that I keep right next to me at my scrapbook table. That thing holds just about everything but the kitchen sink. I love that I can have all my basics nearby plus tons of little doodads and tools that I use a lot. It's neat and compact, too. I'd go crazy without having my basics like adhesives, a craft knife and ruler, scissors and my Ranger Distress Inks right at my fingertips. Plus, I'm always ready to crop on-the-go!

SHEILA DOHERTY

Describe your supply stash. Is it organized?

Define "organized." I'm not organized, but I'm trying. Really, it's just a matter of finding the perfect system for each item, something that will be easy to manage and maintain. For example, I spent three years keeping my ribbon "organized" in a bag. I finally got fed up of having to untangle it. Now the spools and lengths of ribbon are perfectly hung on pegs on a pegboard. If only an epiphany for how to manage my cardstock and patterned paper would strike…

KATHY FESMIRE

What supply do you spend the most money on?

Hello, my name is Kathy, and I am a patterned paper junkie. When I am shopping I end up with a stack of paper every single time. I just purged a stack of paper that I decided I would never use, and it was at least 6" (15cm) high. Even with the recent purge fresh in my mind, I will still add to my paper collection the next (and every) time I go shopping.

CATHERINE FEEGEL-ERHARDT

What is the oddest item in your stash?

Drum roll, please…I keep a wooden cutting board in my rolling crop bag. Really. I yoinked it from my kitchen two years ago when I fell in love with this wonderful hobby. I've trimmed many a piece of paper with a craft knife on top of it. I've also used it to set eyelets and even as a drop cloth of sorts when painting. When I use it, my pages smell like garlic! My crop bag even smells like garlic.

KELLY GOREE

What is your favorite scrapbooking supply? Why?

Chipboard, chipboard, CHIPBOARD! Did I mention, chipboard? I love it, in any shape, any size, any font. It is absolutely one of if not THE most versatile creative supply. You can paint it, sand it, cover it in patterned papers, ink it—anything goes! It even looks good as is. It also adds incredible dimension without bulk or weight.

Describe your supply stash. Is it organized?

I am organized! Actually, it's not hard and kinda fun if you incorporate the organization into your décor. I store all my little embellishments in hardware store nuts-and-bolts containers. I also keep lots of clear jars full of my faves. I love to look at my florals, scrap pieces of ribbon, bling, buttons and whatever fancies me at the moment. All my ribbon is hung on big rings and hangs on hooks, all sorted by color. All my other products are stored right under my scrap counter in labeled drawers.

What is your signature supply?

Brads, brads and more brads. Mini brads, in particular, are a not-so-secret obsession of mine. I continue to buy more for fear I won't have just the right color when I need it. However, when it comes to mini brads, I am quite particular. They must be shiny, have a "flat" top and easy-to-bend prongs. I cannot tell you how many scrap injuries I've gotten from poking my finger with unruly prongs.

What is your favorite scrapbooking supply? Why?

Ribbon! I can't get enough of it! I have every size, type, texture and color that you can imagine. It is versatile, with a million possible uses, and it adds such great texture to my layouts. I am certain that for every unique mood and page theme, there is a ribbon to match.

What supply have you been guilty of overusing?

Chipboard and rub-ons. I love them both. I am comfortable using them. Why stop a good thing? But, I do like a little adventure in my chipboard and rub-on world. For example, often I will slice the rub-ons into new shapes and wonder how the rub-on designer would feel about the fact that I have no intention of using them as intended. I do love a little artistic license.

What is your favorite scrapbooking supply? Why?

Wow! I really have to narrow it down to one? I guess my answer would have to be paper. Paper is your foundation; it sets the mood for the entire layout. It's also one of the least expensive supplies. It sounds corny, but for about 60 cents you can buy a new canvas on which you paint your memories.

JILL JACKSON-MILLS

What did you love about this project?

I had to create something unique with a glass jar. I love a challenge, but trying to come up with something innovative was truly taxing. I covered the jar with paper first, but I didn't like how rigid and one-dimensional it looked. Faced with another challenge, I decided to cover the jar with fabric, which changed everything for the better. When something doesn't work, just head in another direction and eventually you will arrive.

CRYSTAL JEFFREY RIEGER

What is your signature supply? Guilty pleasure?

Color—I can never get enough color, and even though it is technically not a supply, I work with it most often as a tool to create a mood or a look that I want. I am often experimenting with new color combinations, and nothing gets me more excited than when I find just the right shade.

KELLI NOTO

What supply do you spend the most money on?

I don't tend to spend a lot of money on scrapbook supplies, although my husband might argue otherwise. My expenditures last year? Approximately the equivalent of one round of golf and a ski lift ticket for him. I try to use what is in my stash and keep things pretty basic. I don't go for a lot of bulky embellishments or high-dollar items.

RONEE PARSONS

What did you love about this project?

I created a lot of pages that I wouldn't have otherwise. Normally, my page ideas are borne of the photos, journaling and memory—content drives design. But this time it was the opposite. I focused on the supplies first. It was fascinating! I would think, "what could I do with this?" and then figure out the page theme to complement it. It was hard, but a great challenge.

SUZY PLANTAMURA

What is your signature supply? Guilty pleasure?

I love ink—I tend to ink everything. I can't print a picture without inking the edges with black to give it that finished look and a little texture. I just fell in love with the Cat's Eye Fluid Chalk ink pads by Clearsnap. They work with chipboard so well, and they are much easier to use than paint.

HEIDI SCHUELLER

Describe your supply stash. Is it organized?

Cozy (read: very small) creative studios must be organized—there's not enough room to be messy! My space is eclectic in the sense that nothing matches. The décor was driven by clearance circulars. I have wooden drawer cases from Ikea, a series of slotted paper trays bolted into the wall connected by dowels full of ribbon, plastic storage containers for my embellishments. Repurposed juice containers that I've gussied up hold colorants, and old spice racks house my paints, glues and paper flowers.

TORREY SCOTT

What is the oddest item in your stash?

Hmmm. That is a loaded question. I have broken eggshells, electrical resistors, a 1914 hand-blown glass spifflicator and two entire aisles worth of stuff from Home Depot. I am *the* scrapbooking MacGyver, scrapbooking secret ninja warrior and mad scientist, so I consider it my duty to go where no other scrapbooker would even think, dream or want to go on a layout. Oh, I also have s custom leather holster for my Scotch® ATG adhesive gun by 3M, and I wear it on my hip like a six-shooter. Consider me armed…and dangerous.

KATRINA SIMECK

What do you buy and never use?

Rubber stamps and stamping ink. I love the look of stamping. I have bought so many cool stamps and great inks, but I just haven't achieved great results. I think stamping takes a bit more patience, and a steadier, perhaps less caffeinated hand (I cannot scrapbook without coffee and dark chocolate M&Ms). Patience and steadiness are not exactly my strong suits.

TRUDY SIGURDSON

What is your signature supply? Guilty pleasure?

My sewing machine and distressing ink. If I don't use one or the other, my projects look naked and unfinished to me. I think that a swipe of ink or a row of stitching provides the perfect finishing touch to just about anything I make.

MICHELE SKINNER

What did you love about this project?

I loved being challenged to find original uses for supplies that have been lying around and collecting dust for months, even years. It made me listen more carefully to the little creative voices in my head. At the same time, it was really hard and frustrating, too. I definitely grew as an artist. I think it is important for scrapbookers to challenge themselves creatively; it's the best way to improve your craft.

NICOLE STARK

What supplies do you keep within arm's reach?

Besides the usual adhesives, paper trimmer and pencil? I always keep an American Crafts precision pen for hand journaling, ink pad, bags of buttons, tins of odds and ends and a small accordion file filled with rub-ons, descriptive word stickers, small tags and everything I love to use as finishing touches on my layouts. If I don't keep it within reach, it gets lost in a drawer somewhere. My "must haves" are on a desk shelf, right in front of my face.

SHANNON TAYLOR

What is your favorite scrapbooking supply? Why?

To be perfectly honest, I don't have a favorite supply. I just love embellishments as a whole. I like lots of junk on my pages! Speaking of junk, recently I found an old metal washer in the parking lot of our local grocery store. It had been broken & looked like the letter "C." I used it on a page and loved it! Scrapbookers need to keep their eyes peeled—supplies are everywhere!

DENISE TUCKER

What supply have you been guilty of overusing?

At one point in my scrapbooking career, none of my layouts were complete without embossed and/or textured papers. It progressed and suddenly regular patterned paper and cardstock just seemed too flat. I've recovered, in a sense, but I'm still addicted to the "lumpy" look, so I tend to use a lot of foam adhesive, allowing me to still achieve a dimensional look.

LISA TUTMAN-OGLESBY

What is your signature supply?

No page is complete without a little machine stitching somewhere, and I always find a place to use a little chipboard. I also edge an element with chalk and ink on just about every page, even if it's just a little corner. I love how ink adds a small, subtle, vintage detail.

SAMANTHA WALKER

Describe your supply stash. Is it organized?

My stash is VERY organized…until I start a project. I have a hard time choosing what to use, so I end up with a pile on the table BEFORE I begin to scrapbook. It's embarrassing—I have to have two tables for scrapbooking, yet I often end up scrapping on my lap because those tables are covered with creative supplies. Once I've finished a project, I can't and won't begin another until my room is spotless and everything is vacuumed.

SUSAN WEINROTH

What supplies do you keep within arm's reach?

All of my adhesives must be within reach. At last count that variety totaled an impressive 11. There is no one do-it-all adhesive, but there are a lot of adhesives specifically designed to be perfect for a certain job. I also must have handy my paper trimmer, circle punches, a pencil, paper piercer and felt flowers.

HOLLE WIKTOREK

What do you spend the most money on?

Photography is my largest expense. A great camera, memory sticks, image-editing software, processing costs, and the occasional professional photo shoot can exceed my monthly scrapbooking budget quickly. Not only is photography a monetary issue, but it is also time-consuming. Photos are the key to preserving memories, and I refuse to skimp on time and money in this area.

tools

"Where are they now?"

A phrase saved for the once-hot celebrity is also apropos for many of our scrapbooking tools. You know the ones—they were our trusty companions when we first started scrapbooking but have since been passed over for newer, younger models. As our creative appetites grow, the scrapbooking industry is only too happy to oblige with one-upmanship in the tool category. Our old favorites are forever being infused with trendy features and a promise that the new and improved version will optimize our results. In this chapter, get schooled on what can be done with the tried-and-true. You'll find new uses for your reliable favorites. Nothing trendy. Nothing superfluous. Just a few forgotten tools that deserve to be celebrated.

Deco scissors! I almost forgot I owned them. Give me a reason to dust them off.

Susan Weinroth
Masters 2006

Photo: Kristi Mangan

This page background gets a great dose of creativity from a spiraling pinwheel created from ribbon, felt, rhinestones and buttons. But the secret to the layout's success is the excellent yet subtle use of line, texture and color contrast within the pinwheel. The hard, straight edges of the ribbon are intensified by the zigzag edges of the felt triangles, which are a result from being trimmed with pinking sheers. The zigzag line is echoed in the waving rickrack found on the green and blue triangles. The circular buttons and rhinestones prevent the layout from being too structured.

Supplies: Cardstock; Kraft cardstock; brad, letter stickers (American Crafts); ribbon (American Crafts, Pebbles); buttons (American Crafts, Autumn Leaves); rhinestone flowers (Me & My Big Ideas); rhinestone accents (Junkitz, Westrim); rickrack, trim (Wrights); metal tag (Making Memories); decorative scissors (Fiskars); denim fabric; craft felt; dye ink; Impact font (Microsoft)

Be honest, if we weren't telling you to look for a creative use for deco scissors, would you really notice how cleverly they were used on this page? Various sized squares were cut from polka-dot patterned paper and then trimmed with two types of scallop-style deco scissors. They meld almost seamlessly with the background—the gentle scallop edges of the squares mimic the simple curves of the flower petals in the background paper. By lacing a strand of eye-popping pink string around green brads on top of the layered diagonal design, the squares are happily married to the background paper.

Supplies: Cardstock; patterned paper (SEI); plastic letters (Jo-Ann's); chipboard accents (KI Memories); transparent hearts (Heidi Swapp); acrylic paint, letter stamps (Making Memories); brads; string; decorative scissors (Fiskars); pen

Jill Jackson-Mills
Masters 2007

The natural response when picking up a pair of deco scissors is to use them to cut a straight line. For centuries (OK, years), scrapbookers have relied on their trusty deco scissors to give a little oomph to page borders and photo mats. But, decorative scissors have a much higher purpose—shapes with all types of edges. For example, see what they will do to flower petals. The petals on this page were backed with straightedge leaves for a layered look brimming with contrast.

Supplies: Cardstock; letter stickers, patterned paper (BasicGrey); flower (Queen & Co.); brad (Making Memories); decorative scissors (Fiskars); chalk ink; pen

Jessie Baldwin
Masters 2005

I could use a little confidence in using a craft knife. Would you offer some tips?

once UPON a Time

WES + DADDY READING BOOKS TOGETHER 10/06 OPENING A BOOK IS LIKE OPENING A DOOR,... YOU NEVER KNOW HOW FAR YOU'LL GO, TO KALAMAZOO OR SPAIN.

Nicole Stark
Masters 2007

Craft knives can go where no other cutting tool can. In this layout, the photo appears to be swimming among a sea of flowers and flourishes. These were trimmed ever so carefully from patterned paper. Making such precise cuts will take some practice. For best results, use a sharp blade. These designs required twice changing the blade to prevent snags and knife slips, which can result in injury. Also, as you work around curves, turn the paper to prevent awkward cutting positions. Remember to have the patience to go slow.

Supplies: Cardstock; patterned paper (BasicGrey); buttons (Autumn Leaves, Imaginisce); journaling accents (Heidi Swapp); rub-on accents (Imaginisce); pigment ink; craft knife; pen

No one said you couldn't cut paper stars with scissors, but using a craft knife will absolutely ensure that the corners and tips are perfecto. Simple shapes are a great way to build your craft-knife-wielding skills. They will get you in the practice of making long, straight cuts while allowing you to get comfortable holding the tool. Most creative types will hold the knife just as they would a pencil, but do what works for you. Once these shapes were cut from patterned and solid paper, they were mounted to the background with foam adhesive, adding a fantastic energy to this page.

Katrina Simeck
Masters 2007

Supplies: Cardstock; patterned paper (Autumn Leaves); chipboard stars (Pressed Petals); brads; notebook paper

Craft-knife cuts don't always need to be perfectly straight or precisely linear. In fact, curved cuts add a soft touch that can reinforce a theme such as love or friendship. In this layout featuring a beautiful portrait of husband and wife, the artist used a craft knife to cut various-sized hearts in the bright pink cardstock background. The curvature of the beautiful die-cut title letters support the love theme. If you don't have a die-cutting machine in your arsenal, use your craft knife to hand-cut letters in a delicate and flowing script.

Supplies: Cardstock; patterned paper (AdornIt); die-cut letters (QuicKutz); craft knife; chalk ink; foam spacers

Kelli Noto
Masters 2003

I love my letter stamps, but crave a little more variety in how to use them.

Jill Jackson-Mills
Masters 2007

Sometimes an old favorite could use a little remixing, which is the art of reinvention by cutting, rearranging and adding effects to change the style of the original while maintaining its integrity. In this instance, lettered backgrounds deserve a little reconstructive love. Instead of using letter stamps to fill up an entire canvas of cardstock, confine random letters inside a mosaic design. Twist and turn the letters for a little chaotic energy. This mosaic pattern was cut into a stair step design and the letters were stamped within each box. A matching page border was stamped to help balance the page.

Supplies: Cardstock; letter stamps (Hero Arts); solvent ink; acrylic paint; heart accent (unknown)

Ink implies permanence like few other supplies. That's why stamping can seem so intimidating to scrapbookers. Once you put that stamp and ink to a page, it ain't goin' nowhere. Stamping onto a clear transparency solves that problem. The clear transparency can exist as a subtle layer on a layout, allowing the stamping to seamlessly blend into the design. Once you stamp the word or design, you can also experiment with its placement risk-free.

Lisa Tutman-Oglesby
Masters 2007

Supplies: Cardstock; patterned paper (SEI); letter stamps (Making Memories); acrylic paint; tab (7gypsies); heart brad (Hot Off The Press); photo turn (BasicGrey); word sticker (Pebbles); chipboard heart (Heidi Swapp); rub-on accent (Creative Imaginations); transparency; thread

Titles stamped with super-sized foam letters usually come in two varieties: big, black and bold or big, pastel and distressed. Either style is perfectly fine, but a stamped title that splashes across a page in vibrant color is hard to ignore. The stamped portion of this title stretches across more than half of the page. The rest of the title is also stamped, but is smaller. Its spark comes from a cool illusion. Letters were stamped on punched circles of brown paper with watermark ink and were then layered with foam adhesive over punched circles of patterned paper, causing the brown circles to appear as if they are blooming from the spiraling lines in the patterned paper beneath.

Holle Wiktorek
Masters 2003

Supplies: Cardstock; patterned paper (KI Memories); letter stamps (LaPluma, Making Memories); accent stamps (Paper Salon); circle punch; die-cut heart (QuicKutz); ribbon (Michaels); embossing enamel, sepia ink (Ranger); acrylic paint; foam spacers; watermark ink; pen; Pharmacy font (Dafont)

How can I use my circle cutter to create inspired page designs?

Ronee Parsons
Masters 2007

As scrapbooking evolves as a craft, the unconventional seems less and less strange and more and more interesting. No longer are scrapbook layouts expected to stay within the confines of a 12" x 12" (30cm x 30cm) box. They can stretch the boundaries by daringly hanging over page edges or break out of the box entirely. Take this layout for example: The background is not square at all. Instead, it is a layering of patterned paper circles cut from a circle cutter. This conventional tool created various-sized circles that were assembled in a very cool, unconventional way.

Supplies: Cardstock; patterned paper (Daisy D's, Dream Street, Zsiage); rub-on accent (Daisy D's); letter stickers (BasicGrey); pen

Pigtails on little girls will never go out of style and neither will circles. Use a circle cutter to crop your support photos and computer-printed journaling block for maximum design unity. If used fashionably, polka-dot patterned paper will bring sheer delight to pages. The trick is to use it in small doses and allow the rest of the design to build from it. For example, you could use a colorful print such as the one shown in this layout as part of your foundation, and allow the bubbly polka dots to bounce from the pattern in the form of buttons and other spherical accents.

Sheila Doherty
Masters 2005

Supplies: Cardstock; patterned paper (American Crafts); buttons (American Crafts, Making Memories); brads (Karen Foster); circle cutter; Century Gothic font (Microsoft); MammaGamma font (Dafont)

Why crop photos into circles? Because it's a great way to really zero in on the focal point of the photo—the tight boundaries of a circle, unlike those of a rectangle or square, eliminate all unwanted peripherals. Grouping a series of circles can also free up space on a layout. The photos on this page were effortlessly cropped with a circle cutter, which allowed the artist to crop the photos in a variety of sizes. The focal photo is, naturally, the largest of the bunch.

Hillary Heidelberg
Masters 2007

Supplies: Cardstock; letter stickers (Making Memories); number sticker (American Crafts); rub-on accents (7gypsies, Die Cuts With A View); Arial journaling font (Microsoft); Suede title font (Internet download)

What are the best advantages for using a die-cutting machine?

My baby turned five today.

Why does this make me so sad?

FIVE

I just want her to stay little forever!
She promises me she will still give me
lots of hugs and kisses
and sleep with me at night.
She will always be my baby in my heart,
but I guess it's time to get
to know my big girl! 03/06/07

Suzy Plantamura
Masters 2006

If your page design calls for a series of identical shapes, a die-cutter is a natural choice.
First, it makes cutting shape after shape a breeze. Second, and more importantly, it ensures that
the shapes are going to be exact and uniform. In this layout, the word "five" was die-cut from a
sheet of cardstock the same shade as the one that was used for the background. Repeating the
word gives the layout subtle dimension and reinforces the title, also cut from the same paper
and letter dies, but distinguished with inky edges and raised with foam adhesive.

Supplies: Cardstock; patterned paper (Paper Adventures); die-cut letters (Provo Craft); buttons, rickrack (Doodlebug); digital frame
(Two Peas in a Bucket); chalk ink; dimensional adhesive; pen

When it comes to creating a background for a scrapbook page, die-cutting machines are an obvious yet overlooked choice. Often, scrapbookers will reach for their alphabet stamps or pristine sheets of newly-purchased patterned paper before thinking, "Gee, how cool would it be to create something fabulous from scrap paper?" The next time you are in a design rut or the monthly scrapbooking-supply budget has run out, grab the die-cutting machine and wander over to your scrap heap. Chances are good you'll come up with something equally as awesome as this background, which was created with a couple of tag dies. After the tags were punched and adhered in an orderly fashion to the back of the page, holes were punched in the top of each tag and a brad was inserted (another great way to use up a supply that scrapbookers own by the hundreds).

We aren't the same people we were when we met in college in 1992. We've been through too much together. We've had so many years. We've adapted to each other. We've assimilated with each other. We love more, fight less, compromise often. We laugh things off. We finish each other's thoughts and sentences. No, we aren't the same people. We're better.

Michele Skinner
Masters 2007

Supplies: Cardstock; patterned paper (BasicGrey); die-cut tags (QuicKutz); chipboard letters (Zsiage); brads (American Crafts); Apple Garamond font (Internet download)

The die-cutting machine employed to create this layout is not your mother's die-cutting machine. Before, scrapbookers were limited to using the dies manufactured for their die-cutter of choice. Some of today's die-cutting machines can be connected to a computer, which empowers them to cut most any shape or, in this case, in any computer font. Once the lettering was cut in the desired font, the words were adhered to the page background along the right side of the page. The result is the look of a hand-cut font in much less time.

Supplies: Cardstock; decorative snap, patterned paper (We R Memory Keepers); cutting system (Wishblade); Babel Sans journaling font, Amaze title font (Internet downloads)

You are such a sweet little kit, Julian. You absolutely adore your Babar and Celeste animals. These were actually gifts to your brother when he was born, but he never found them terribly interesting, so we put them on a high shelf and forgot about them. When you were born, Julian, we pulled them off the shelf, not really expecting that you would play with them. But by one year old, it was clear that you were not the same child as Luca...not by a long shot. You insist on sleeping with Babar and Celeste in your crib. You often can be found placing Babar in your booster seat and feeding him bananas or crackers. You like to put them "to bed", and are always sure to give them a kiss and cover them with a blanket. It makes me smile to see the love and affection you give to them. You're definitely unique, your own little person, Julian.

(January 2007)

Babar & Celeste

Hillary Heidelberg
Masters 2007

Why is the corner rounder such a fantastic tool to own?

DAY THREE
60 miles completed.
All in a 3-Day's work.

the story

I Walk ... for my Mom! for my Sister! for my daughters! for my friends! ... There Will be a CURE! I believe!

149,864 STEPS

Catherine Feegel-Erhardt
Masters 2007

This page pays tribute to this artist's feat of participating in, surviving and finishing (in the top 100, no less) a 60-mile, 3-day walk to benefit breast cancer research. Catherine's mother is a six-year survivor, so she walked in her honor as well as for friends, other survivors, others affected and even her own daughters. We could say that the use of the corner rounder on this page is symbolic of the full circle that this artist has come, but really its employment answers a simpler cause: to soften the layout. Catherine's sweet victory is conveyed with distressed patterned papers, sanded and inky edges and a few feminine touches. The rounded corners are a perfect choice for showing a layout's softer side.

Supplies: Cardstock; patterned paper (A2Z Essentials); chipboard numbers (EK Success); acrylic paint; corner rounder (Creative Memories); letter stamp (Little Black Dress); journaling accents (7gypsies, Heidi Swapp); foam adhesive; ribbon (Michaels, Offray); staples; sandpaper; pen

Every scrapbooker should own a corner rounder. It is a popular way to finish a layout because it can add design unity in a subtle way. On this layout, the corner rounder was used on the photos, photo mat and on all four pieces of patterned paper. The rounded edges of these otherwise rectangular elements soften them and tie them together, helping the eye move smoothly across the layout. The rounded corners also complement the distressed circles in the polka-dot patterned paper used for the background.

Lisa Tutman-Oglesby
Masters 2007

Supplies: Cardstock; patterned paper (BasicGrey); corner rounder (Marvy); flowers (Making Memories, Prima); letter stickers (Chatterbox); charm (Jo-Ann's); chipboard clock (Heidi Swapp); chipboard stickers (EK Success); brads; die-cut photo turn (QuickKutz); epoxy sticker (K&Co.); circle cutter; thread; transparency

Corner rounders: used for creating curves or tiny triangles? Yep. Corner rounders are indeed intended to round corners. But, when you use them, not only do you wind up with curved corners, you also are left with tiny triangular scraps, the remnants of the very corners you rounded. These little triangles are handy—use them as photo corners, borders or as little arrows to direct the eye, which is how they have been used on this layout.

Sheila Doherty
Masters 2005

Supplies: Cardstock; patterned paper (Scenic Route); letter stickers, rub-on accent (BasicGrey); corner rounder (Creative Memories); acrylic paint; swirl accent (7gypsies); pen; BastardusSans, Dear Joe II fonts (Dafont); design elements (Adobe)

I'm thinking about tossing my paper punches. Should I reconsider?

A set of paper punches in basic shapes is über practical. Use these paper punches to cut a series of repeating shapes, which can then be used to create an easy background or a set of cute little accents. Or, punch some quick photo corners, tags, page borders, labels, and, well, we could go on, ad nauseum. These are all very positive ways in which to use your punches, but have you ever thought about using them in a negative way? To create negative space that is. Here, circles were cut FROM the background and a piece of cardstock was layered beneath so the white would peek through. The leftover punched circles were then inked and added to the layout for a wee bit of dimension.

Supplies: Cardstock; beads, brads, chipboard letters (Queen & Co.); circle punch (EK Success); transparent snowflakes (Heidi Swapp); pigment ink; pen

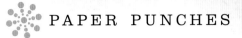

Circle punches were used to create original accents that are just as yummy as the donut in this photo. To mimic the rainbow sprinkles, circles were cut from sheets of clear transparency. To give them definition, acrylic paint was squeezed around the edges of the clear plastic. Once dry, the accents were secured to the layout with small stitches atop a border created from folded and stapled lengths of ribbon. Epoxy letter stickers composing the title give the layout a candy-coated feel.

Crystal Jeffrey Rieger
Masters 2007

Supplies: Patterned paper (KI Memories); transparent folder (Staples); circle punch (Marvy); acrylic paint; thread; epoxy stickers (unknown); ribbon (Michaels); staples; pen

It's not just the circle punches that deserve a second look. Square punches can be used alone or combined to great effect. Here, square punches of two different sizes were used in tandem to create frames that were then woven together. First use a 1⅜" (3.5cm) punch to make the outside of the frame, then use a 1" (3cm) punch to punch out the center. The small photos in this layout may have gotten lost, but the entertwined frames, set on a slightly different angle, make them pop.

Supplies: Patterned paper (My Mind's Eye); square punches (EK Success); letter stamps (Li'l Davis); chalk ink; thread

Andrea Vetten-Marley
Masters 2004

Are fonts and other digital dynamite causing templates and stencils to become obsolete?

With the popularity of fonts and the ease and thriftiness with which they can be acquired, our poor lettering templates are left to collect dust. On the practical side, templates can be used to trace and cut letters from scrap paper, which is not always an option when printing. The letters for this title were cut from a template and then stitched to the layout. Trace and cut the letters slightly larger than their outline to accommodate the stitching. Use temporary adhesive to place the letters onto the layout and pre-punch the stitching holes with a paper piercer. When finished, thread your needle and stitch away.

Christine Brown
Masters 2005

Supplies: Patterned paper (Mustard Moon); letter stickers (BasicGrey); lettering template (EK Success); chipboard shapes (Fancy Pants); buttons (Autumn Leaves); thread; patterned transparency (Creative Imaginations); journaling tag (Making Memories); rub-on accents (American Crafts); stamping ink; pen; Chelt Press font (Internet download); Georgia font (Microsoft)

When scrapbookers speak of "embossing," 9 out of 10 times they are referring to heat embossing. Dry embossing is rarely seen on scrapbook pages, which is a shame because it's a great way to add easy yet interesting dimension. To dry emboss, you will need a stencil and a stylus. Place the stencil onto the back of a piece of paper and use the stylus to trace the design. Once finished, flip over the paper and enjoy your raised image. For extra dimension, lightly sand the embossed design.

Supplies: Cardstock; brass stencils, patterned paper (Lasting Impressions); rub-on accents and words (Heidi Grace); decorative scissors; mulberry paper; vellum

Lisa Tutman-Oglesby
Masters 2007

Templates and stencils make it possible for everyone to be an artist. They allow the effortless creation of shapes and lettering styles that some otherwise would not be able to draw or write. On this stacked layout a template was used to create the swirls. The template features a collection of delicate curves. The templated curve shapes were combined to custom create the swirls seen on the layout.

Supplies: Cardstock; patterned vellum (My Mind's Eye); patterned transparency (unknown); patterned paper (KI Memories); chipboard letters (Scenic Route); letter stickers (Doodlebug); stencil template (Die Cuts With A View); pen

henry nailed his form.

and he easily broke his board.

and he kicked butt in sparring.

Michele Skinner
Masters 2007

but the look of pride on his face when he got his black belt?

that was the best part of the night!

12.2.06

I have a couple of different types of eyelet setters. Help me to put them to good use.

What an awesome fairwell dinner at Ohana's Restaurant in Disney World.

The food was delicious and the entertainment was kid friendly.

However, sharing it with the best of company made it a "magical" night!

December 2006

Heidi Schueller
Masters 2003

Eyelets are a great way to increase the unity factor on a page. They are unobtrusive, so you can repeat them on a layout without distracting from the photos, journaling or title. The floral accents on this layout needed an extra punch to give them some flower power. Eyelets were added to the centers of all of the flowers. The larger flowers benefit from the added petal details the eyelets provide.

Supplies: Patterned paper (Crafter's Workshop, Frances Meyer); chipboard flowers (Frances Meyer); mini eyelets (Making Memories); large eyelets (unknown); eyelet setter; paper flowers (Prima); rub-on words (One Heart One Mind); Toms New Roman font (Internet download)

Eyelets can be intimidating accents. After all, they do require a hammer to be installed. If you suffer eyelet anxiety, simply set out (pun intended) to create a layout such as this. The tranquil photo mandated a tranquil page design. The spiraling eyelet design exceeds that goal by adding understated color and interesting dimension. To create such a spiral, place a photo in the middle of the page. On scratch paper, draw a template for the curved eyelet design and repeatedly trace onto the layout background to create a spiral. Set a straight line of eyelets on the edge of each curve and freeform set the rest to fill in the shape.

Crystal Jeffrey Rieger
Masters 2007

Supplies: Patterned paper (Fancy Pants); eyelets (Making Memories); eyelet setter; pen

Layouts are always in need of a finishing touch. Sometimes that touch comes in the form of a doodle or a few well-placed swirls. Using an eyelet setter to create straight, zigzag or curvy line designs will give a layout a good dose of "pop." The design on this page connects two strips of patterned paper with holes created from eyelet setters of different sizes. The holes also cradle the journaling and the pink cardstock under the holes adds a splash of unexpected color.

Supplies: Cardstock; patterned paper (Paper Salon); rub-on accents (Die Cuts With A View); eyelet punch; Franklin Gothic Medium Condensed, SP Purkage fonts (Internet downloads)

Hillary Heidelberg
Masters 2007

I love my label maker, but what are a few artistic ways in which to use it?

What would you do with a thin strip trimmed from a photo? If you're Torrey, you'll try running it through your label maker! That's just what she did for the journaling on this layout. For the background text, vellum was cut into strips and run through just as you would the regular label tape. Sand the papers a little to make the letters pop. Here she stretched the labels across the photo, resulting in a funky look that detracts not a bit from the photo.

Torrey Scott
Masters 2003

Supplies: Cardstock; patterned paper and cutouts (Cosmo Cricket); label maker (Dymo); vellum; brads; chalk ink; sandpaper; adhesive foam

Labels might just be the hardest working scrapbooking supply. At least they are on this page. Not only do they reinforce the journaling, they also help connect the photos to each other as well as provide color and line-quality contrast against the background. By repeating the question, "can we feed the fish," the incessant chirp of a young child's wishes is cleverly conveyed.

Nicole Stark
Masters 2007

Supplies: Patterned paper (Daisy D's, KI Memories); letter stickers (American Crafts); label maker (Dymo); photo corners (Heidi Swapp); dictionary paper; pen

Using a label maker to print
journaling captions is nothing new,
but the way in which this label-made
journaling was created is certainly
intriguing. The shiny look of labels
would have been out of place on
this collage-inspired layout; the
slickness of the labels would have
appeared too manufactured for the
beautifully artistic and rough-edged
piece. Instead, Ronee placed vellum
over the labels and rubbed the words
with a black crayon to achieve the
utilitarian lettering perfect for this
layout.

Supplies: Cardstock; die-cut letters, patterned
paper (Daisy D's); letter stickers (Arctic Frog); label
maker (Dymo); gel medium; vellum; crayon

Ronee Parsons
Masters 2007

HOW'D SHE DO THAT?

1 Punch the journaling with the label maker
and adhere to another piece of paper.

2 Place a sheet of vellum on top and rub
a crayon across it to pick up the raised
surface of the punched letters.
Adhere the vellum to the page.

I'm thinking of buying a sewing machine. What are some easy ways to add machine stitching to layouts?

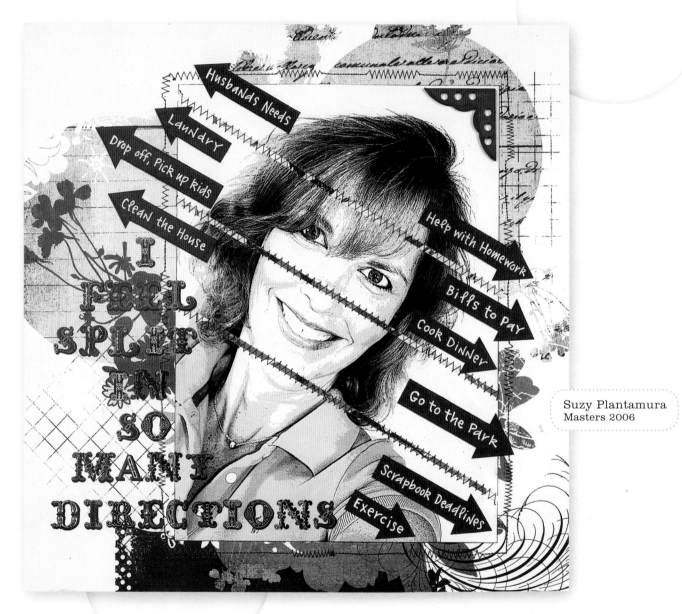

Suzy Plantamura
Masters 2006

While stitching normally adds a certain warmth and homeyness to a page, it can also add a frenzied feeling. The photo depicts Suzy's smiling face, which she tries to maintain despite the hectic life she leads as a mother. Machine stitching runs across the page, divvying up the photo. The directional zigzags of the stitches are too symbolic of this too busy life. They reinforce the journaling, which details all of Suzy's daily responsibilities on fire-engine red arrows that also give the page a sense of urgency.

Supplies: Cardstock; patterned paper (BasicGrey); rub-on letters (Fancy Pants); thread; chalk ink; solvent ink; pen

If you are going to use fabric on a scrapbook page, why not sew it? Obviously, machine stitching and fabric go hand-in-hand, but there are practical benefits as well. Fabric that is machine-stitched to a page requires no stabilizing. Also, you will, by and large, achieve much neater results with stitching than with adhesive. Furthermore, you can be sure that fabric stitched to a page has a much smaller chance of becoming unattached. On this page, a generous block of denim was easily stitched to a piece of cardstock. It makes the perfect backdrop for baby boy photos.

Katrina Simeck
Masters 2007

Supplies: Cardstock; patterned paper (Imagination Project); chipboard letters (Pressed Petals); letter stickers (Arctic Frog); button (Autumn Leaves); rickrack; brads; denim fabric; thread

Machine stitching enjoys many practical uses in scrapbooking, but sometimes it simply says, "homemade," "warm," "touchable" and "comfy." Pages about family ties especially can benefit from a little sewing here and there. For this page, squares of coordinating patterned paper were cut and then stitched to the layout background. The result is a quilted look, perfect for the coming together of three dear sisters.

Catherine Feegel-Erhardt
Masters 2007

Supplies: Cardstock; patterned paper (SEI); thread; letter stickers (Mrs. Grossman's); rub-on accents (Making Memories); fibers (American Crafts, Offray); pigment ink; adhesive foam

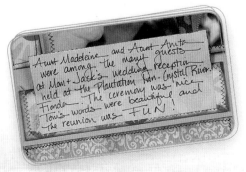

STALE supplies

"Leftovers, again?!"

Many a parent has heard that dreaded sentence uttered from a whining child or spouse in response to a quick-and-easy dinner. As scrapbookers, we often feel a similar pain and sentiment when evaluating our scrapbooking supplies. It's hard not to when so many new supplies are paraded before us at the scrapbook or hobby store, online and in scrapbooking magazines. We must get over this feeling and develop a deep appreciation for our basic supplies. Let's not roll our eyes at our paper collections, adhesives and colorants. No, let's celebrate them for the creative opportunities they permit us. They are the staples of our hobby and without them, well, it would be almost impossible to scrapbook.

I love my patterned paper, but sometimes struggle with using it elegantly. Can you help?

Susan Weinroth
Masters 2006

Use your patterned paper to create an original super-sized motif. Scrapbooking is a paper craft, so you no doubt have gads of scrap paper lying around, just waiting to be used. Collect a pile of coordinating pieces, trim into strips and cover a shape, such as a large heart. It's an easy and creative way to add a personal, unique and homemade touch to your layout. The base of the heart was cut from cardstock. Once the strips were adhered to the top, the edges were trimmed. For dimension, the heart was adhered to the layout with foam adhesive.

Supplies: Cardstock; patterned paper (BasicGrey); buttons, rub-on accents (American Crafts); chipboard letters (Heidi Swapp); brads (Queen & Co.); rickrack (Wrights); floss; SP Zuppa Toscana font (Scrapsupply)

THE LIGHT

When shopping, it is easy to be seduced by patterned paper. Papers sing a siren's song, calling out with their bold patterns and bright colors. But once you get home, how do you use papers that feature large motifs, high-contrast colors and intense patterns? Use them judiciously; otherwise, they will overpower a layout. On this page, a sheet of bright patterned paper is only just visible between gutters of space trimmed into a piece of white cardstock, helping to frame the page and the photo.

Supplies: Cardstock; patterned paper and transparency (Hambly); craft knife; journaling accents (unknown); pen

Ronee Parsons
Masters 2007

Contrast—whether you are juxtaposing two different things or highlighting the difference between lightness and darkness—is key in creating interesting designs. When working with patterned paper, set brightly colored sheets against a solid black background for an intense look. On this layout, a mix of colorful patterns was used to create the title and the pattern-blocked background.

Supplies: Cardstock; patterned paper (My Mind's Eye, Scenic Route); chipboard letters, ribbon (We R Memory Keepers); buttons (unknown); pen

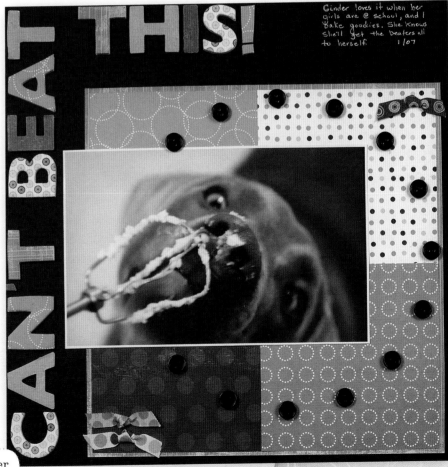

Heidi Schueller
Masters 2003

43

Can you challenge me to be more creative with cardstock?

Shannon Taylor
Masters 2005

Paper-only layouts sound boring, but they can be amazing. Again, creating paper-based layouts will force you, as a designer, to showcase the photo in an incredible way. This design really zeroes in on the photo. The round shape of this boy's hat-sporting head made cropping the photo into a circle a natural choice. It was placed just below and to the right of the page center (this placement is a great design secret for attracting the eye). The circle shape was repeated by creating a circle frame from black cardstock strips. The frame was then energetically filled with circles punched from patterned paper scraps.

Supplies: Cardstock; patterned paper (unknown); chipboard letters (Heidi Swapp); circle punch; foam adhesive; Milkshake font (Two Peas in a Bucket)

If you want to give your creative juices a real challenge, create a layout with photos, journaling and cardstock. It seems limiting, but you might surprise yourself with texture techniques. This page's success comes from repeating a simple scallop edge. Cardstock with decorative edges is now available, and the scallop edge is popular and easy to find. A notch-and-die tool and hole punch were used to create the black scalloped cardstock strips that echo the scalloped heart design.

Supplies: Cardstock (Bazzill, Provo Craft, WorldWin); letter stickers (Doodlebug); transparent letters (Heidi Swapp); notch & die tool (BasicGrey); hole punch (Karen Foster); staples; string; pen

Kelly Goree
Masters 2006

A page that is strong on design needs little embellishment. Remember that the next time you want to head to the store to buy more cute, little doodads. Little more than cardstock was used to create this page celebrating the arrival of a new family member. A wall of photos was cropped to create a wave on which the title rides. This gives the page movement and energy. The title was also cut from cardstock, and the giant No. 2 helps anchor the design.

Supplies: Cardstock (Bazzill); letter stickers (Arctic Frog); brads; Bullet Balls, Wendy Medium fonts (Internet download)

Hillary Heidelberg
Masters 2007

Give me three reasons to pull out the shrink plastic I bought years ago.

Sheila Doherty
Masters 2005

Shrink art works fantastically for titles. You can draw on shrink plastic, stamp the letters, or trace a font. If you want your letters to be as big as Sheila's, you'll have to print them at a large point size (remember, they will shrink!). Once printed, these letters were a whopping 8" (20cm) high. Cut out the letters and trace onto shrink plastic. Using solvent-based ink, stamp the word "joy" on the letters and color them in with colored pencils. Trim the letters from the shrink plastic and bake according to package instructions.

Supplies: Cardstock; patterned paper (American Crafts); shrink plastic (Shrinky Dinks); letter stamps (FontWerks); colored pencils; solvent ink; Asinine, Porcelain fonts (Dafont); Impact font (Microsoft)

Shrink plastic rocks because you can do so much with it. You can paint it, stamp on it and even print on it. The charms on this page were created with a little digital dynamite, and they are easy, fun and very cool. For these charms, scan a favorite piece of patterned paper. (Tip: You may want to use image-editing software to adjust the color, brightness or saturation because colors will intensify once you bake the shrink plastic.) Print the image onto a sheet of shrink plastic and then use circle and flower punches to cut out shapes from it. Punch smaller holes into the circle centers to mimic the look of buttons. Bake the shapes according to package instructions. Once cool, embellish with rickrack and ribbon.

Supplies: Cardstock; patterned paper (ANW Crestwood, Collage Press, K&Co., Scenic Route); shrink plastic (Shrinky Dinks); buttons, ribbon (Making Memories); circle template, decorative punches (EK Success); decorative scissors; pen; Century Gothic font (Microsoft); Wendy Medium font (Internet download)

Michele Skinner
Masters 2007

You can create any kind of dimensional element with shrink plastic. Here, a frame was created. Trim the edges of an 8½" x 11" (22cm x 28cm) sheet of shrink plastic with decorative scissors and cut out the frame window with a craft knife. Punch ¼" (6mm) holes along the border. Bake according to package instructions. Shrink plastic has a tendency to curl when baking; this can be remedied by covering the plastic with a sheet of parchment paper while baking. Once the shrink plastic comes out of the oven, you can use your fingers to gently flatten any curled pieces while it is still warm. When cool, lace embroidery floss through the holes.

Supplies: Patterned paper, die-cut flower (My Mind's Eye); shrink plastic (Grafix); ribbon (Michaels); felt; floss; hole punch; pen

Crystal Jeffrey Rieger
Masters 2007

I am aware of the conventional uses for transparencies, so give me some interesting ideas for using them.

Preprinted transparency frames are the latest and greatest way to enhance your photos. Many times they are almost completely transparent, containing just enough creative detail to draw attention to your photo without distracting from it, unlike a big, honkin', opaque frame. This elegant focal photo benefits from two transparent frames. The frames were layered so their paisley designs would overlap. By stapling the frames to the layout, no messy adhesive shows through.

Jill Jackson-Mills
Masters 2007

Supplies: Patterned paper (7gypsies, BasicGrey); patterned transparency (My Mind's Eye); die-cut letters (BasicGrey); staples

Transparencies have as many creative uses as they have practical uses (for example, use a transparency sheet to protect the glass bed of your scanner from scratches and dust).

On this page, alcohol ink was drip-dropped onto an inkjet transparency sheet to create a wild overlay. Vinyl letters were arranged on the rough side of the sheet to act as masks for the ink (the rough side will hold the ink and vinyl stickers so they will cling to the transparency; otherwise the ink will spread under the letters). Once everything dried, the letters were removed, leaving the negative spaces to spell out the message.

Crystal Jeffrey Rieger
Masters 2007

Supplies: Cardstock; inkjet transparency (Staples); ribbon (Michaels); alcohol ink; buttons (American Crafts); vinyl letters (unknown); foam adhesive; pen

A transparency's goal in life is to be see-through, so it is a wonderful tool for layering, encapsulating items and, of course, for making windows. This purse will make you want to shake it (the purse itself and perhaps your bootie) because of the shaker-boxes it has across the front of it. Three square openings were cut from the purse and then backed with a square of cardstock that was cut slightly larger than the opening. Beads were deposited inside and the openings were then covered with a transparency square. The purse was covered with cardstock, which had been trimmed to allow the bead boxes to show through.

Samantha Walker
Masters 2005

Supplies: Purse (unknown); patterned paper, rub-on accents, transparencies (Creative Imaginations); flowers (Prima); beads (Provo Craft); decorative scissors; pen

Clear glaze is often used as an adhesive, but are there ways to use it more creatively?

Catherine Feegel-Erhardt
Masters 2007

Cruises. Beach scenes. The pool. Sprinkler sessions. These are all page topics that will benefit from a little clear glaze. Why? Because you can mimic the look of water! On this page, well-placed clear glaze complements the watery photo and page theme. Circles were cut from patterned paper, shadowed with cardstock and glazed. Clear glaze adds depth to the spirals on the red patterned paper, helping accentuate the circular shape of the setting sun and the ripples in the water. The clear plastic letters in the title also get the gloss, making them appear almost as blue as the water.

Supplies: Cardstock; patterned paper (A2Z Essentials, Cosmo Cricket); glossy dimensional adhesive (Ranger); transparent letters (Heidi Swapp); letter stickers (Creative Imaginations); ribbon (American Crafts, BasicGrey); staples; sandpaper; stamping ink; pen

When you want just a hint of shimmer, clear glaze is the bomb. It's pretty easy to use, given any caffeine or sugar you have ingested isn't causing your hands to quake. Plus, it's lightweight. But, a really cool trick for using clear glaze is to make custom accents with it. First, you need a nonstick surface. Plastic wrap or wax paper will do. Secure the wrap or wax paper to a flat surface and make sure there are zero wrinkles. Grab your glaze and draw. Once dry, peel the glaze and adhere to your page. In this example, circles were created, but use your imagination!

Crystal Jeffrey Rieger
Masters 2007

Supplies: Patterned paper, ribbon, rub-on accents (SEI); letter stamps (Paper Salon); punctuation stamp (Technique Tuesday); dimensional adhesive (Ranger); stamping ink; leather scraps (unknown); pen

If you love the look of epoxy stickers, try your hand at making your own with an image and clear glaze. Clip art was used on this layout, but you could also use a stamped image or even a freehand drawing. Print art on white cardstock, cut into circles and adhere to chipboard (this will prevent the paper from curling once the glaze is applied). Apply two thick coats of glaze, allowing the first to dry before the second application. Once the second coat is dry, add your new embellishment to your layout.

Supplies: Cardstock; patterned paper (unknown); diamond glaze (JudiKins); chipboard tags (Making Memories); floral border (Doodlebug); clip art images (Microsoft); corner rounder

Jennifer Bourgeault
Masters 2004

I never grow tired of foam adhesive, so please show me some great layouts featuring it.

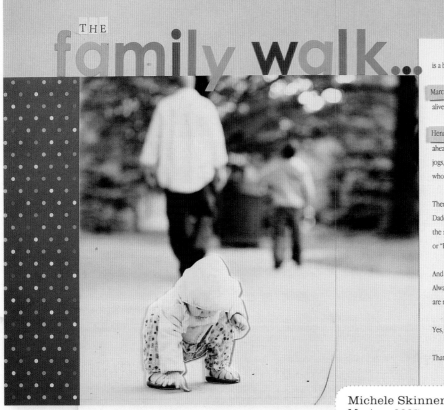

THE family walk...

is a bit of a misnomer.

Marc forges ahead, goal in mind. Keeping the spirit of adventure alive. Keeping the troops in line.

Henry comes next, characteristically inconsistent. He runs up ahead. He falls way behind. He darts right and left. He skips, he jogs, he does a crazy little boneless wiggle walk. And he talks the whole time.

Then there's Harper. 20 little toddler steps for every one of Daddy's 6'4" stride. Frequent stops to examine a rock. A crack in the sidewalk. A leaf. Frequent stops to exclaim, "Plane!" or "Bug!" or "Flower!" Frequent stops just to stop.

And bringing up the rear is Mom. Always behind the family. Always snapping the shot. Always watching to make sure the kids are moving forward. And not into the path of oncoming vehicles.

Yes, we take walks. But family walks?

That all depends on what you mean by "family."

Michele Skinner
Masters 2007

What do you get when a creative mind combines a compelling photo, foam adhesive and spot color? A super cool image with a totally "look at me" focal point. This technique works best with photos that have a distinctive foreground subject plus a little activity in the background from which to distinguish it. Print two copies of a photo—a color and a black-and-white copy. Silhouette cut the focal point from the color copy and layer over the black-and-white copy with foam adhesive. Sit back, ooh and then ahh.

Supplies: Cardstock; patterned paper, sticker accent (SEI); letter stickers (Making Memories, SEI); foam adhesive (3M, Therm O Web); corner rounder; Apple Garamond Light font (Internet download)

Without foam adhesive, this all-paper layout would be exceptionally flat. But with foam adhesive, the layout is exceptional.
The spiraling journaling captions warranted the first dose of foam to prevent the flower design from being too static. A few more circles, the photo and the tag also get the treatment. The lifted elements cast shadows, which mimic the shadows in the photo as well. Inky edges add even more dimension and texture.

Supplies: Cardstock; die-cut tag, letter stickers, patterned paper (Paper Salon); foam adhesive (Therm O Web); thread; staples; chalk ink; pen

Catherine Feegel-Erhardt
Masters 2007

The use of foam adhesive is perfect for this page showcasing several in-your-face photos of the family dog. The page background was lifted from the scallop-edge cardstock, as were several of the smaller squares that house photos of the pup and other fun embellishments. Inky edges and an eclectic collection of embellishments combine to give this quirky page spirit.

Supplies: Cardstock; label sticker, patterned paper (7gypsies); chipboard letters and shape (We R Memory Keepers); foam adhesive (Ranger); foam stamp (Junkitz); rub-on accent (Cosmo Cricket); metal pin (Around the Block); ribbon (May Arts); brads; eyelets; tags (Avery); embossing enamel and powder, alcohol inks, metallic mixative, memory foil tape, archival ink; distress ink (Ranger); domino, flowers, magnet word, linen thread (unknown); pen

Lisa Dixon
Masters 2004

How can I take heat embossing to the next level?

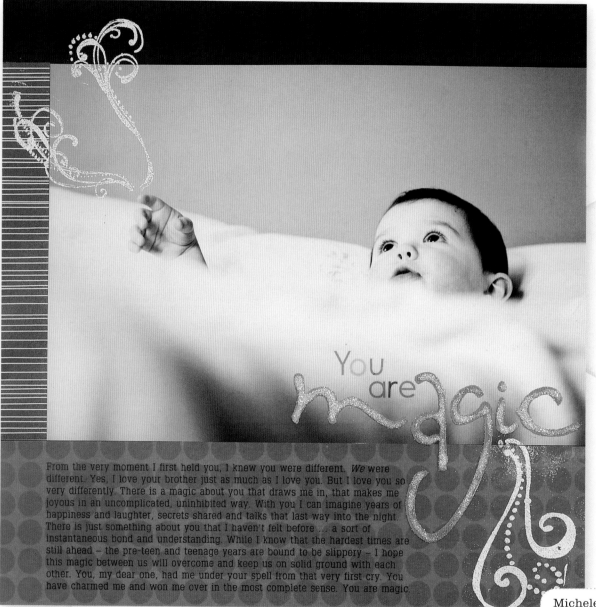

From the very moment I first held you, I knew you were different. *We* were different. Yes, I love your brother just as much as I love you. But I love you so very differently. There is a magic about you that draws me in, that makes me joyous in an uncomplicated, uninhibited way. With you I can imagine years of happiness and laughter, secrets shared and talks that last way into the night. There is just something about you that I haven't felt before ... a sort of instantaneous bond and understanding. While I know that the hardest times are still ahead – the pre-teen and teenage years are bound to be slippery – I hope this magic between us will overcome and keep us on solid ground with each other. You, my dear one, had me under your spell from that very first cry. You have charmed me and won me over in the most complete sense. You are magic.

Michele Skinner
Masters 2007

First there was traditional scrapbooking with paper, scissors and glue. Then there was digital scrapbooking with a computer, and the digital scrapbookers were (and are) developing techy techniques to mimic the look of paper pages. Now, traditional scrapbookers are mimicking the look of the digital dynamos. Can you say, "full circle?" This page features delicate swirl motifs that are all the rage in the digital realm. Digital scrapbookers use brush tools from image-editing software to create them. On this page, stamps and embossing powder were used. Stamp a swirl with watermark ink and heat emboss with glittery embossing powder.

Supplies: Cardstock; patterned paper (KI Memories, My Mind's Eye); stamps (Autumn Leaves); embossing powder (JudiKins); glitter; pigment ink; rub-on letters (KI Memories); Smitten Kitten, Typo Slab Serif Light fonts (Internet downloads)

When scrapbooking sports, we often think of the dirt, the sweat, the rough and the tumble. Rarely do we pay attention to the shinier side of athletics. Looking at a football jersey, it's easy to see that shiny side, and heat embossing is a great way to complement it. Almost every bit of blue on this layout was heat embossed—the title letters, the edges of the layout, the staples on the football element and the football charm. The chipboard title letters were first sprayed with crackle-finish spray paint and, once dry, with blue stained-glass spray paint. After they dried, they were heat embossed for a helmet-like finish. To heat emboss the edges of the layout, strips of double-sided tape were adhered to the edges and then sprinkled with blue foil embossing powder and heated.

Denise Tucker
Masters 2004

Supplies: Cardstock; patterned paper (Freckle Press, Rusty Pickle); transparency (Kodak); digital photo and paper protectant, crackle top coat (Krylon); chipboard letters (Rusty Pickle); decorative staple bars (EK Success); sport charm (K&Co.); stamping inks; embossing powder (Plaid, Ranger, Stampendous); foam adhesive; Dateline font (Internet download)

Back in the old days, scrapbookers had to use big, bulky inkpads to apply embossing ink to surfaces. Times were tough! There weren't any new-fangled, fancy pens that would allow crafters to apply embossing ink anywhere they wanted. No! They had to work for their shiny heat-embossed results. Dramatics aside, this layout's inky edges and freeform doodling were embossed with the help of an embossing pen. Apply embossing ink where desired and then sprinkle with embossing powder. Shake off excess, heat and show off your art to others.

Ronee Parsons
Masters 2007

Supplies: Cardstock; patterned paper (Daisy D's, SEI); rub-on accents (Daisy D's); embossing powder (Jo-Ann's); paperclips; pen

I would love some ideas for incorporating mesh into my layouts.

just not the same

Willow's Beach, April 2006

Tia, you were such a sweet and loving dog that you were happy to do anything as long as you were with us. One of your favorite things to do was to go to the beach with us and we loved to take you there. You loved to run around and sniff all of the rocks and seaweed and chase after bits of driftwood that we'd throw for you and you loved to make friends with the other dogs who were also out for walks with their owners. Now that you're gone our trips to the beach just won't be the same with out you . . . it just won't be the same.

Trudy Sigurdson
Masters 2003

Mesh can be that "little extra something" you add to pages that have a distressed feel. This page theme largely centers on the beach, and aging and distressing techniques are great for lending a real beachcomber feel. Most elements on this page were inked, sanded and/or whitewashed. Mesh was added as an overlay of sorts to help connect all of the elements.

Supplies: Cardstock; corrugated cardboard; chipboard letters (Heidi Swapp); die-cut letters (QuickKutz); wire mesh, metal washers (local hardware store); dye ink; chipboard hearts (Maya Road); acrylic paint; brads (Scraptivity); staples; Ransom Group Antique font (Internet download)

Mesh can add complete cohesion to a layout. Fabric with a mesh texture gives this layout a classic feel and soft touch. The edges of the photo were sliced to create strips (note: the strips are still connected to the photo). These strips were then carefully woven into the fabric mesh. Beads were threaded onto wire and manipulated into a delicate strand of leaves that also were woven into the fabric mesh.

Supplies: Cardstock; mesh fabric (Hobby Lobby); fabric (Wal-Mart); beaded wire (Wrights); word beads (Darice)

Andrea Vetten-Marley
Masters 2004

Mesh is largely a textural supply, but it can certainly be thematic as well. Stop and think for a moment, where does mesh texture occur in your life? Screen doors. Football goal posts. Beaches. And, of course, fishing nets.
On this page, a 12" x 12" (30cm x 30cm) sheet of mesh was trimmed to have a scallop edge and adhered to the background to insinuate that the entire layout was inside a net.

Supplies: Patterned paper (BasicGrey, Crate Paper); mesh (Magic Mesh); letter stickers (Three Bugs in a Rug); word stickers (Pebbles); chipboard heart (Heidi Grace); epoxy sticker (K&Co.); thread; acrylic paint; circle punch; pen

Lisa Tutman-Oglesby
Masters 2007

I suddenly realized that I have quite a collection of paint. What are some of your favorite ways to use it?

Acrylic paint and chipboard go together like peanut butter and jelly. Chipboard, with its porous texture, sturdy construction and thickness was made to be painted. Although chalk and stamping ink are wonderful colorants to use with chipboards, they just don't give you the saturation of acrylic paint. Plus, if you want to cover large areas of chipboard with color, acrylic paint is a much more efficient choice. Chipboard letters and a chipboard tag were swabbed with acrylic paint on this layout. The uneven paint application works well to add dimension and enhance the texture. Acrylic paint was also used with clear plastic letters. The letters were applied to the background as a mask, painted over and, once the paint dried, removed for a spray-painted effect.

Diana Graham
Masters 2003

Supplies: Patterned paper, decorative tape, tab (KI Memories); chipboard letters and stars (Fancy Pants); acrylic frame, journaling accent, photo corner, word masks and tags (Heidi Swapp); acrylic paint; brads (Making Memories); pen

For peek-a-boo painting, use a mask. Masks can be used with any colorant, but their most popular companions are acrylic paint and stamping ink. Color is applied over a mask to create a negative image. For this layout's mask, a leaf motif was cut from a piece of patterned paper and temporarily adhered to a piece of white cardstock. Three colors of paint were brushed over it. Once the paint dried, the mask was removed and the title was stamped on top with foam outline stamps. The stamped letters were then cut from the paper and outlined for definition.

Supplies: Cardstock; patterned paper (K&Co., Urban Lily); mesh (Magic Mesh); acrylic paint; letter stamps (Li'l Davis); circle stamps (Making Memories); clock accents (Heidi Swapp); circle accents (Creative Imaginations); brad

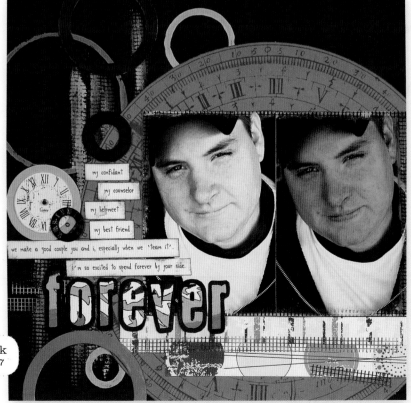

Nicole Stark
Masters 2007

FINGER PAINTIN

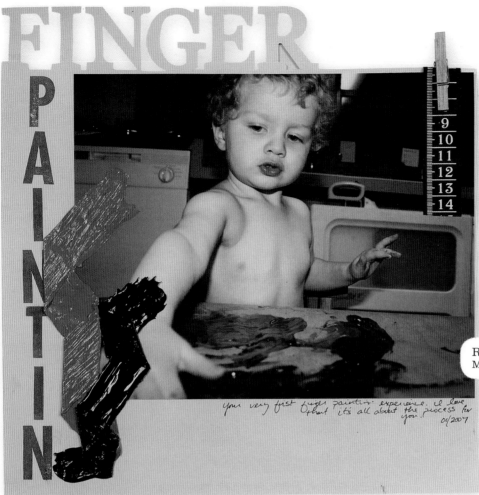

Finger painting is a rite of passage for every child that should be captured in every mother's scrapbook pages. Use the clever technique shown here to mimic the look of globs of finger paints on your layout.

Supplies: Cardstock; letter stamps (Paper Salon); pigment ink; acrylic paints; decorative tape (7gypsies); clothes pin; pen

Ronee Parsons
Masters 2007

your very first finger paintin' experience. I love that it's all about the process for you! 04/2007

HOW'D SHE DO THAT?

1 Paint several coats of liquid acrylic paint onto a plastic bag, allowing each coat to dry before the next is added. Continue to apply coats until the paint is about ⅛" (3mm) thick.

2 Once the paint is dry, peel the strip from the plastic.

3 Form the paint strip into the desired shape, in this case, curled. Allow the paint to harden, then adhere it to the page.

Resist techniques are probably easier than I think, right? Please show me.

Kelly Goree
Masters 2006

When trying to create a resist, remember that pretty much any waxy surface will resist color. Take, for example, crayons. Crayons can be used to draw and color on pages, and they will resist most any color applied over them. On this layout, an adorable piece of art from Kelly's son was used as the base of a watercolor resist. She asked her son to create a mini masterpiece over which she carefully painted with blue watercolor. Once dried, she adhered the joint creation to the layout.

Supplies: Cardstock; patterned paper (BasicGrey); letter stickers (BasicGrey, Doodlebug); chipboard accent (Queen & Co.); acrylic paint; crayons; watercolor paint; corner rounder; pen

Lisa Tutman-Oglesby
Masters 2007

This is an example of a true resist. A resist is simply a design, usually stamped and heat embossed, that repels, or resists, any color that is applied over it. On this layout, four resists were created. Circles were cut from cardstock, stamped upon using resist ink (you can also use watermark ink) and heat embossed. Then, each was given a color wash with spray ink and the excess ink was carefully removed from the embossed design. The embossed, stamped image now emerges from the bed of color as a delicate design.

Supplies: Cardstock; patterned paper (American Traditional, Flair Designs, Scenic Route, Sweetwater); chipboard letters (Fancy Pants, Heidi Swapp); color wash ink, embossing powder, relief ink (Ranger); rub-on letters and accents (K&Co., My Mind's Eye); corner rounder; circle cutter; acrylic paint

Did you know that stamping with resist ink on a piece of solid cardstock will create a watermark? It is a great way to add subtle pattern to layouts. On this layout, a flourish stamp was used with resist ink to create delicate flowers. Small paper flowers were centered inside the flourishes for embellishments that add just the right touch of femininity to this layout.

Supplies: Cardstock; patterned paper (Daisy Bucket); flowers (American Crafts); brads; stamps (Autumn leaves); resist ink (Ranger); pen

Katrina Simeck
Masters 2007

61

How can I put the "fun" into functional when using tape?

i love the LOOK in YOUR EYES! i love the LOVE in YOUR Heart! Eva @ 5

Catherine Feegel-Erhardt
Masters 2007

Tape can add wonderful texture and color to layouts. If you visit an art supply store, check out the selection of artist and graphic tape. You'll find tapes with shine and sheen, tapes with a matte surface, tapes with an almost fabric touch and tapes of all widths. Artist tape was used on this layout. Painters use the tape to mask the edges of canvases or to help them paint straight lines. It was used on this layout to create a spiraling design element (trim the tape into sections and overlap to help create smooth curves). It also shows up in the journaling and as a page border.

Supplies: Cardstock; patterned paper (A2Z Essentials); tape (3M, Heidi Swapp); sandpaper; foam adhesive; pen

These little beauties are definitely the fairest of them all! They must be if their scrapbooking mother created this layout with handcrafted beaded flowers for them. The most important ingredient of these flowers is double-sided tape because it gives them an invisible background and the utmost security. Trace flowers onto the backing of double-sided tape (or punch them with a flower punch). Peel off one side of the backing, add a button in the center and sprinkle with beads, gently pressing them into place with your finger or a brayer. Remove the other backing and apply to your layout.

Supplies: Patterned paper (Fancy Pants, One Heart One Mind); rub-on accents (Making Memories, One Heart One Mind); beads (JewelCraft, Queen & Co.); pearls (Westrim); paper flowers (Prima); pink and green buttons (Die Cuts With A View); black buttons (unknown); fibers; Zots Dots, Memory Tape Runner, Peel n Stick adhesive (Therm O Web); Leroy Brown, Whackadoo fonts (Internet downloads)

Heidi Schueller
Masters 2003

Masking tape was used in a fairly traditional manner on this layout. The obvious use is the journaling strips. Masking tape historically has been used for labeling items, so it naturally accepts ink very well. The tape was also used to protect the layout. The mesh-textured stars were achieved by layering a star cut from mesh on top of the layout and then rubbing an ink pad over it. To hold the mesh star steady and to protect the layout from errant ink swabs, it was taped to the layout with masking tape.

Nicole Stark
Masters 2007

Supplies: Cardstock; patterned paper (Imagination Project); chipboard letters (BasicGrey); letter stickers (Making Memories); mesh (Magic Mesh); chipboard heart (Heidi Swapp); masking tape; pigment ink; adhesives (3L, Therm O Web, Tombow); pen

Rub me the right way with your ideas for using rub-ons.

Feeling alive & completely carefree...

Remembering to live in the moment...

And most importantly...

FUN

On a perfectly sunny afternoon last summer.

(Photo July 2006 in Florida)

Susan Weinroth
Masters 2006

Photo: Kristi Mangan

Transparencies are thin and delicate; when you apply rub-ons to a transparency, the result is a seamless accent. Rather than being an overlay, the transparency is the base of this layout. After the rub-ons were applied, a thick blue cardstock frame was cut to fit over top of the transparency. Green ribbon was then stitched to the inner edge of the frame and blue lace was used to trim the frame as well. The frame was adhered to the transparency and then the photo was added. Journaling strips were mounted with foam adhesive and fabric letter tags complete the layout.

Supplies: Cardstock; transparency (Office Max); ribbon, rub-ons (American Crafts); felt flowers (Paper Source); letter tabs (Scrapworks); vintage lace; pigment ink; thread; SP Strut font (Scrapsupply)

Just as versatile as chipboard, rub-ons are a must-have in your scrapbook arsenal. Pair the two for the incredible results. This large chipboard ampersand was just begging to be played with. So, its wish came true when it was painted a lovely green. Once dry, beautiful and delicate rub-ons were applied, and the once plain, brown ampersand now has the look of quaint bed-and-breakfast wallpaper.

Supplies: Patterned paper, rub-on accents (BasicGrey); buttons (Autumn Leaves); jumbo ampersand (Making Memories); letter stickers (American Crafts); thread; marker

Shannon Taylor
Masters 2005

Nicole Stark
Masters 2007

Rub-ons are many a scrapbooker's weakness. But as far as weaknesses go, they are a good one to have because rub-ons are so versatile and so easy to use. On this page, a variety of holiday rub-ons were applied to the edges of the background, taking ordinary cardstock and transforming it into a wonderland of patterned paper.

Supplies: Cardstock; patterned paper (BasicGrey); letter stickers (Three Bugs in a Rug); rub-on words (Making Memories); sticker accents (7gypsies)

Who doesn't have gobs of stickers? Please help me use some of mine!

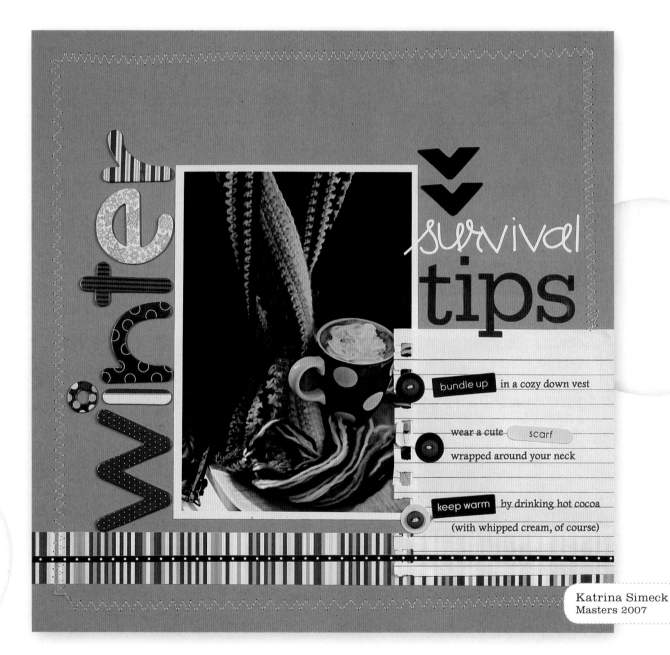

Katrina Simeck
Masters 2007

Journaling is a natural place for sticker usage. The journaling block on this layout gets a punch of color and contrast with a few strategically placed sticker phrases. The black and red stickers pop off of the white journaling block background and help enhance the other instances of red and black that appear on the layout.

Supplies: Kraft cardstock; chipboard letters, patterned paper, sticker accents (KI Memories); letter stickers (American Crafts); buttons (SEI); notebook paper; thread

believe

iNEXPLiCaBLE JOY

I thought I knew what joy was a few years ago when I did a layout called "Finding Joy". But you know what? I didn't. I didn't at all! When I found joy before it was because I had found Jesus. And I was indeed experiencing a new life in Christ, new with his Spirit. But as joyful as I thought I was, I didn't yet know what being truly joyful meant.

The thing I've learned these past two very difficult years is that joy does not come from happiness. Joy is a process and it leads to happiness. But finding true joy is not easy. It does not come when you're walking down rose-lined streets with the sun shining on your face, being cheered on by an adoring crowd.

It comes instead after you've walked many miles down a muddy and slippery road that winds seemingly aimlessly through treacherous forests and thorny bushes, an ominous sky overhead threatening to strike you down at any time.

It comes after you've cried and prayed and cried and prayed and cried some more. After you've all but given up. . .left with no choice but to give it over to God. It comes after you're finally able to look outside yourself, past all the self-pity, hurt, anger and frustration. It comes after you open your eyes to see all the ways God is working in your life, even through your circumstances. It comes after you finally come to recognize His grace and protection in your life… it's the knowing and feeling His presence around you!

Now, after all these things, I finally know true joy!! The kind described in the Bible… truly INEXPLICABLE JOY!!! Joy that follows me wherever I go and sustains me regardless of my circumstances! I now know with ALL confidence that as long as I remain faithful and live in His Word, God will reward me with joy untold!!

Blessed is the man who perseveres under trial, because when he has stood the test, he will receive the crown of life that God has promised to those who love him. James 1:12

What you consider trash a Master might consider treasure. The title for this layout was created from a leftover sticker sheet. When you pull up a sticker from its backing paper, a negative shape is left. Creative use of these shapes double your pleasure because you get maximum use from your sticker purchase. Cardstock stickers are especially great because many times, the negative space retains a color outline left by the original sticker. Here stickers were cleverly used on the flower petals, too.

Supplies: Patterned paper (My Mind's Eye); letter stickers, rub-on accents (BasicGrey); photo corners (Heidi Swapp); buttons (Autumn Leaves); foam adhesive; Times New Roman font (Microsoft)

Christine Brown
Masters 2005

Designing an action-packed layout such as this can seem intimidating, but it's not because the kinetic design was contained within the confines of imaginary blocks. Look at the layout and see if you can divide it into blocks of information. There are four basic blocks, the most obvious being the title and the photo (included in the photo block is the recipe for the yum-yums pictured). The other two blocks exist on the top and left side of the photo; they compose the journaling. Balancing groups of descriptive-phrase stickers and the ingredient list created the journaling.

Supplies: Cardstock; patterned paper (SEI); sticker accents (7gypsies); chipboard letters (Zsiage); Times New Roman font (Microsoft)

Jill Jackson-Mills
Masters 2007

NOT-SO-NEW
embellishments

"Keep the romance alive!"

Let's face it: We have a relationship with our scrapbook embellishments. They are the fun-loving wonders of the scrapbooking world that set our creative hearts aflame. When we first meet a trendy embellishment, it's a total honeymoon phase. The mere sight of the little doodad on our scrapbook table makes us giggle, and we can't use enough of our new flame on our pages. But then the magic starts to fade. We still love and purchase our embellishment hottie, yet the once explosive creative potential has become stale. This leaves us vulnerable to the next hot stud of the scrapbooking world, and thus the cycle begins again. The first step to breaking the pattern is to use what you have before buying anything new. It will be a healthy challenge.

What are some easy-peasy ways to use beads on my layouts?

Ronee Parsons
Masters 2007

Think of beads as a dimensional colorant, adding spunk and shine to your pages. On this layout, a beaded flower element commands much-deserved attention. The flower accent was trimmed from double-sided tape and adhered to the layout. Beads were sprinkled on top and then a brayer was used to smooth the design.

Supplies: Cardstock; patterned paper (Crafter's Workshop, Dove of the East); beads (Darice); rub-on accents (Daisy D's); dye ink

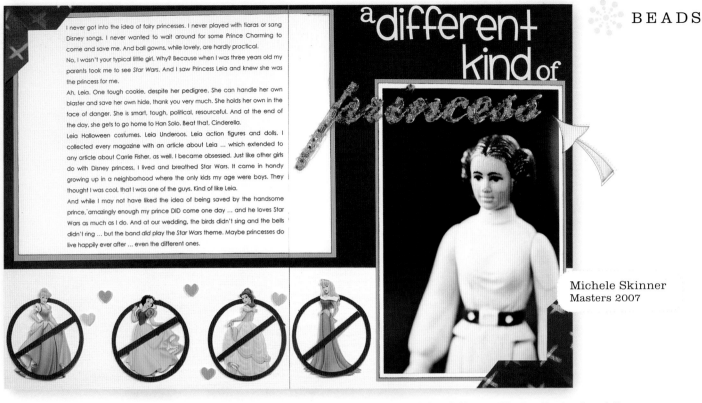

a different kind of princess

I never got into the idea of fairy princesses. I never played with tiaras or sang Disney songs. I never wanted to wait around for some Prince Charming to come and save me. And ball gowns, while lovely, are hardly practical.

No, I wasn't your typical little girl. Why? Because when I was three years old my parents took me to see Star Wars. And I saw Princess Leia and knew she was the princess for me.

Ah, Leia. One tough cookie, despite her pedigree. She can handle her own blaster and save her own hide, thank you very much. She holds her own in the face of danger. She is smart, tough, political, resourceful. And at the end of the day, she gets to go home to Han Solo. Beat that, Cinderella.

Leia Halloween costumes. Leia Underoos. Leia action figures and dolls. I collected every magazine with an article about Leia ... which extended to any article about Carrie Fisher, as well. I became obsessed. Just like other girls do with Disney princess, I lived and breathed Star Wars. It came in handy growing up in a neighborhood where the only kids my age were boys. They thought I was cool, that I was one of the guys. Kind of like Leia.

And while I may not have liked the idea of being saved by the handsome prince, amazingly enough my prince DID come one day ... and he loves Star Wars as much as I do. And at our wedding, the birds didn't sing and the bells didn't ring ... but the band did play the Star Wars theme. Maybe princesses do live happily ever after ... even the different ones.

Michele Skinner
Masters 2007

Try mixing beads with a favorite font for exciting results. Fonts with thicker letters will give the best results. Reverse-print a title onto an inkjet transparency (you can use patterned paper or cardstock as well, but the transparency will give you a clear background). Cover the printed words with clear-drying craft glue and sprinkle with beads. Smooth the beads with your finger or a brayer (make sure the beads stay within the font outline to ensure readability) and let dry. Add a finishing coat of clear glaze to set the beads.

Supplies: Cardstock; patterned paper (KI Memories); letter stickers (Doodlebug); sticker accents (EK Success); solvent ink; beads (unknown); circle template; diamond glaze (JudiKins); liquid pearls (Ranger); Century Gothic font (Microsoft); Porcelain font (Internet download)

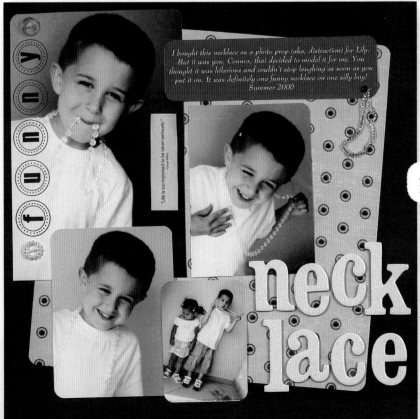

If creating a full-on beaded embellishment seems daunting, use beads sparingly to add shine and dimension. Here, beads were centered in the middle of the polka dots on the patterned paper background. A small beaded necklace was also created to support the page theme.

Jennifer Bourgeault
Masters 2004

Supplies: Cardstock; patterned paper (unknown); beads (Westrim); chipboard letters, pearl accent (Li'l Davis); rub-on letters (unknown); rub-on quote (K&Co.); brad; corner rounder

When my pages call for glam, glitter is key, but how can I use it with less mess?

Glitter applied so deftly only could have come from the hands of a Master, right? Well, yes, a Master did create this artwork, but the technique is super simple because of the specialty rub-ons used. Once applied, these rub-ons have a slightly tacky surface so that glitter sprinkled on top will stick. No messy glue or clumpy glitter glue.

Supplies: Cardstock; glitter, glitter rub-ons, patterned paper (K&Co.); chipboard flowers (Fancy Pants); ribbon (American Crafts); thread

Vanessa Hudson
Masters 2006

"Bling"—so many things to so many people. In this case, Kathy's daughter called her new cell phone her "bling." And a glittery, girly layout was born. For hints of glitter anywhere on your layout, use a paintbrush to brush decoupage medium onto the corners of photos or chipboard letters, even onto silk flowers and buttons. Then bring on the glitter.

Supplies: Patterned paper (BasicGrey, My Mind's Eye); chipboard letters (K&Co.); chipboard accent (BasicGrey); letter stickers (Old Time Pottery); rub-on accents (American Crafts); glitter, ink, decoupage medium (Plaid); silk flowers (Teters); floral charms (Crafts Etc.); ribbon (Offray); sequin flowers (Queen & Co.); brads; buttons; transparency

Kathy Fesmire
Masters 2004

Glitter can be used to glitz up a preprinted design. A screen-printed transparency overlay got a glitter makeover on this layout. See how it was done in the steps below. A clear-drying dimensional adhesive was used on this layout to give the finished design some depth. Once the glue and glitter are dried, carefully add a finishing coat of clear-drying glue to set the glitter in place.

Supplies: Cardstock; patterned paper (Daisy D's, Scenic Route); transparency (Hambly); glitter (Making Memories); chipboard letters (Chatterbox); corner rounder; sandpaper; paper bag; staples; pen

Catherine Feegel-Erhardt
Masters 2007

HOW'D SHE DO THAT?

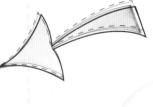

1 Using a clear-drying glue with an applicator tip, fill in a section of the printed area of the transparency.

2 Sprinkle ultra fine glitter over the transparency. Once the glue is dry, tap off the excess glitter.

When it comes to rhinestones, it's a thin line between classy and tacky. How can I use them to my best advantage?

This page appears to catch a falling star, and it proves that rhinestones can and do find a home on boy pages. To re-create the look, draw or trace a shooting star design onto your page background. Use tacky adhesive dots to secure rhinestones within the design. The result is a shimmery sleepy-time page with dimension and movement.

Supplies: Cardstock; rhinestones (Westrim); letter stickers (Making Memories); rub-on accents (BasicGrey); pen

Rhinestones make a statement, whether used sparingly or with reckless abandon. Here, they were applied to the patterned paper flower centers for a hint of shine and dimension. A few flowers were trimmed from another piece of patterned paper and adhered to the layout with foam adhesive for dimension.

Supplies: Cardstock; patterned paper (BasicGrey, Making Memories); chipboard letters, rhinestones (Heidi Swapp); letter stickers (Chatterbox); word stickers (EK Success, Heidi Swapp); butterfly stickers (K&Co.); chipboard flowers (BasicGrey); small flower (Making Memories); acrylic paint; foam adhesive; thread

Lisa Tutman-Oglesby
Masters 2007

When placed inside the center of a silk flower, rhinestones add playful luster. Smaller flowers were placed in the center of the white silk flowers and the rhinestones were placed in a circular formation around it. They also were used to highlight chipboard swirls.

Supplies: Clipboard frame, rub-on stitching (7gypsies); cardstock; flowers, rhinestones (unknown); ribbons (American Crafts, May Arts); chipboard accents (Maya Road); metallic paint (Li'l Davis); die-cut shapes (QuicKutz); photo anchors (Creative Impressions); brads; glitter glue; chalk ink; letter stamps (PSX)

Trudy Sigurdson
Masters 2003

So many brads, so little time...what are some totally cute ways to use them?

Kate & Mark's adorable new baby boy, Wyatt... Looking cute as can be! Photo November 2006.

Susan Weinroth
Masters 2006

Brads are perfect little circles and as such, they add spice to any design. When creating a title, border or stand-alone design element, think about using brads. Here, the brads give pop and dimension to the title and a circular design element. Trace a title (you could also use a font or write it freehand) and cover with brads (this title is especially cute because multicolored brads were used). For the circular design element, a funky motif was cut from patterned paper and accented with brads.

Supplies: Cardstock; patterned paper (We R Memory Keepers); brads (Queen & Co.); buttons, letter sticker, ribbon (American Crafts); epoxy stickers (KI Memories); metal tag (Making Memories); pinking shears; floss; Florida-TS font (My Fonts)

Brads? There are brads on this page? Actually, yes, there are, only you can't see them because they are hidden under the flowery support photos of this tiny baby. For these cute flower accents, trim flowers from patterned paper (you could also punch or create freehand flowers). Adhere the flowers to the page background and accent with stitches if desired. Trim photos to fit on the head of a large brad, adhere and affix to the center of the flowers.

Shannon Taylor
Masters 2005

Supplies: Cardstock; patterned paper (BasicGrey); letter stickers (American Crafts, BasicGrey); brads (Bazzill); floss; ribbon (unknown); diamond glaze (JudiKins); circle punch; pen; Two Peas Basic font (Two Peas in a Bucket)

Cute mini brads were used to create a whimsical design on this layout that champion's Hillary's good fortune of being camera-ready while her son was pulling a few faces. The color scheme was inspired by the silly one's striped shirt. A star was cut from a sheet of orange paper and adhered to the background with little brads. The star also has a stem of brads that was shaped into an adorable curlicue.

Supplies: Cardstock; patterned paper, sticker border (KI Memories); brads (Queen & Co.); 2Peas Airplane font (Two Peas in a Bucket); Tuffy font (Internet download)

Hillary Heidelberg
Masters 2007

What are some charming ways to dangle elements from my pages?

Katrina Simeck
Masters 2007

Dimension floats on this page like falling snow. Snowflake rub-ons were applied to clear acrylic charms on this layout. The circle charms were framed inside chipboard circles ascending from a concentric design inspired by the patterned paper. The result is a page full of soft movement and gentle flow.

Supplies: Cardstock; patterned paper (Fancy Pants); acrylic charms (One Heart One Mind); chipboard letters (Zsiage); chipboard circles (Imagination Project); brads; rub-on accents (BasicGrey, Fancy Pants); ribbon (Offray); corner rounder

As long as it dangles, almost anything can be transformed into a charm. With the simple addition of a jump ring, photo turns, mini tags and letter accents are transformed from everyday scrapbook supplies into funky wearable art. Look closely to see if you can decipher the following words on the charm bracelet: inspire, dream, create, art, joy, cherish. Catherine's favorite is the word "master," which she spelled with letter stickers on clear, plastic charms.

Catherine Feegel-Erhardt
Masters 2007

Supplies: Bracelet, jump rings (Darice); clear letter tiles; frame charms; letter charms, photo holders, word charms (Jo-Ann's)

Families, Valerie says, come together much like the pieces of a patchwork quilt, the different pieces maintaining their individuality while comprising a greater whole. This layout was designed to resemble such a quilt. Charms were added to help unify the design, add dimension and reinforce the theme of family and faith.

Valerie Barton
Masters 2003

Supplies: Patterned paper (Daisy D's); letter stickers, vellum quote (Colorbök); number stickers (EK Success); charms (Watchfaces-Charms); epoxy stickers (Miss Elizabeths); floss

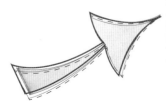

I need to be more daring when creating with buttons. What do you suggest?

It's a very rare occasion when I don't see that lovely face of yours alive with expression. I caught you so deep in thought and peacefulness that I became frozen in my spot. What on earth were you thinking at that moment? What were you feeling? What was going on inside that head of yours to have you so deep in thought? I realize that everyone needs quiet time to themselves, yet I was still taken aback to see such a young, lively and vivacious kid actually experiencing such serenity. When I look at this picture of you I feel tranquil, calm and thankful that the turbulence of the day slowly subsides.

Most true happiness comes from one's inner life... It takes reflection, contemplation, and self-discipline.
William L Shirer

Jill Jackson-Mills
Masters 2007

When your layout calls for small punches of color, reach for your buttons. Here, hot pink buttons echo the color that shouts from the journaling block, ribbon border and patterned paper. Flower motifs were cut from the patterned paper and used to accent the layout. Buttons were added to a few flower centers for more pop.

Supplies: Cardstock; patterned paper (KI Memories, Urban Lily); clear buttons (unknown); colored buttons (Jo-Ann's); clear frames (Making Memories); floss

on the shore

With a song in her head and a dance in her heart, Cameron is truly a free spirit. She danced this little jig on the beach off Lake Huron in Ontario, Canada while visiting Aunt Paula. Of course, only Cameron knows for sure what silent tune prompted this sweet routine. All we do know for sure, is that Cameron definitely moves to the beat of her own drum… and that makes her all the more adorable.

Buttons are wonderful accents that add color and dimension to layouts. Here, they were used in a very subtle way to reinforce the colorful story and add dimension. They are most noticeable across the top of the page where they have been used to accent the centers of the circular motif on the patterned paper. They also appear across the border that waves along the bottom of the photo and on the super-size chipboard letter.

Supplies: Cardstock; patterned paper (K&Co.); chipboard letter (BasicGrey); buttons (Autumn Leaves); die-cut shapes (My Mind's Eye); charms (Darice); flowers (Prima); brads; chipboard circle (Bazzill); acrylic paint; chalk; thread; transparency

Lisa Tutman-Oglesby
Masters 2007

While buttons can certainly be used as a stand-alone accent, you can use several of them to create cool, original accents. On this layout, buttons were used to create intricate-looking flowers. A large green button was picked for the center and then further accented with a smaller blue button and beads. To create the petals, small purple and red buttons were used. Buttons were also used to accent handmade paper flowers and on their own to add hints of color.

*We put the sprinkler on in the backyard so you could play in the water.

*We put a generous coating of sun block all over you. It was hot.

*You changed clothes several times. Each time they got wet, infact.

*The last time you changed your clothes you forgot your t-shirt.

*You ate a raspberry ice block. It stained your tummy.

*You stopped me as I walked past with the camera. "Take a pic-cha of me!"

January 7th

Supplies: Cardstock; chipboard number, patterned paper (Scenic Route); letter stickers (American Crafts); rub-on letters (Making Memories); rub-on accents (BasicGrey); buttons (Autumn Leaves); beads (Queen & Co.); solvent ink; glass finish topcoat (Plaid); adhesive foam; pen

Nic Howard
Masters 2005

What are some absolutely creative ways to use spiral clips, of which I have gobs?

Nicole Stark
Masters 2007

With cute dimensional flowers, spring has definitely sprung on this layout. A spiral clip, created from a single coil of metal wire, looks like a spring. If you use pliers to pull on the inner coil, you will get an actual lightweight spring that can be used to create dimension on a layout. Here, the springs were adhered to the backs of clear plastic flowers, which were cut from a piece of product packaging. To keep the adhesive hidden, buttons were placed on the centers of the plastic flowers.

Supplies: Cardstock; patterned paper (Creative Imaginations, Urban Lily); transparent letters (Heidi Swapp); buttons (Doodlebug); tags (Avery); pigment ink; staples; spiral clips (unknown); acrylic paint; dictionary paper; transparency; pen

Don't send a circle to do a square's job. Decorative paper clips are one of the cooler ways to attach small items to layouts, and round spiral clips are readily available. But sometimes your layout design calls for squares. It's easy to reshape the round clips into square spirals using needlenose pliers. Once these clips were reshaped, they were set to work, attaching a sweet journaling caption to the photo and as a decorative element in the upper-left corner.

Supplies: Patterned paper (Cosmo Cricket, Dove of the East); mesh (Magic Mesh); spiral clips (unknown); chipboard letters (Zsiage); die-cut tags, rub-on accents (Daisy D's)

Ronee Parsons
Masters 2007

Administrative assistants from coast to coast love how spiral paperclips can add a sense of style to humdrum office documents, but scrapbookers love them for the style they add to layouts. Of course they have plenty of practical applications, such as affixing tags, photos, journaling and more to pages, but they can be used as purely decorative elements as well. On these cards, spiral clips were used to build a snowman, help a flower bloom, create a pumpkin and add some pizzazz to a collection of stars.

Supplies: Cardstock; patterned paper (American Crafts, Die Cuts With A View, Pressed Petals, Scenic Route); brads, spiral clips (Creative Impressions); ribbon (Hobby Lobby, Offray); die-cut letters and shapes (QuicKutz, Sizzix); stamping ink; chalk and sepia ink; sponge; snow accent (Aleene's); acrylic paint; foam adhesive; Pharmacy font (Dafont)

Holly Wiktorek
Masters 2003

I find using a stapler on my layouts intriguing—how do the Masters do it?

Catherine Feegel-Erhardt
Masters 2007

Forget about staples being an office supply. Start thinking of them as little strips of metal that can be used to accent your page. They give this layout a boyish, teen-angst energy. If you are wondering how to get a stapler to reach the depths of a layout, keep in mind you have to be resourceful. On this page, most of these staples were added to the tag and photo before these elements were adhered to the background.

Supplies: Cardstock; patterned paper (A2Z Essentials); staples (Swingline); tags (Making Memories); labels (Dymo); sandpaper; chalk ink; silver leafing pen (Krylon)

Staples are all about fun and function on this page. Their purposely imperfect application definitely adds to the boyish feel of the layout, but they also solve a lot of adhesive headaches. For example, ribbon will certainly stay put when you staple it to the background. Staples also keep the photo in place (and, wow, what an interesting way to make a photo corner). The middle of the photo was left unattached so a journaling tag could be slipped between it and the page background.

Supplies: Cardstock; patterned paper (My Mind's Eye); chipboard letters (Heidi Swapp); chipboard accents (BasicGrey); staples; ribbons, rub-on accents (American Crafts); linen (Li'l Davis); dye ink

Kathy Fesmire
Masters 2004

Scrapbookers who are afraid of needles probably aren't keen on stitching. But, if it's stitching they crave, they can use staples instead. Staples criss-cross each other along the edges of this page to mimic cross-stitches. The result is a fun and funky design.

Supplies: Cardstock; patterned paper (7gypsies, Daisy D's, Imagination Project); letter stickers, rub-on accents (Arctic Frog); staples (Swingline); pigment ink; labels (Dymo); pen

Brooke Bartimioli
Masters 2007

I use chipboard every day, but could use a fresh idea or two.

Michele Skinner
Masters 2007

Chipboard is a super-cool accent, but have you ever considered building a background with it? It's easy. Pick a piece of patterned paper and find chipboard accents that complement the style; the ornate swirls and big serif letters of the chipboard chosen for this layout are lovely companions to the organic pattern and distressed painterly feel of the paper. Arrange the chipboard as desired and add a photo on top.

Supplies: Cardstock; patterned paper (My Mind's Eye); chipboard elements (Fancy Pants); ribbon (May Arts); magnetic closure (BasicGrey); watermark ink; foam adhesive; Another Typewriter font (Internet download)

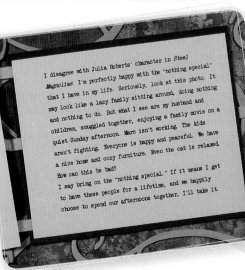

I disagree with Julia Roberts' character in *Steel Magnolias*. I'm perfectly happy with the "nothing special" that I have in my life. Seriously, look at this photo. It may look like a lazy family sitting around, doing nothing and nothing to do. But what I see are my husband and children, snuggled together, enjoying a family movie on a quiet Sunday afternoon. Marc isn't working. The kids aren't fighting. Everyone is happy and peaceful. We have a nice home and cozy furniture. Even the cat is relaxed. How can this be bad?

I say bring on the "nothing special." If it means I get to have these people for a lifetime, and we happily choose to spend our afternoons together, I'll take it.

The letters C,T, and R . . . they look like random letters from the alphabet. But together these letters stand for "Choose The Right." A very important reminder to so many people around the globe.

Wes just received his first CTR ring from church. He came home all excited and now proudly wears the little green emblem on his finger. Every time I see it I can't help but smile.

Remember little buddy . . . always Choose The Right!

Chipboard has a gazillion scrapbooking applications and, therefore, is one of scrapbooking's most revered supplies. As far as chipboard goes, super-sized chipboard letters definitely rule. On this layout, white chipboard letters were used for the title, "CTR," which is an acronym for "Choose The Right." This message is detailed in the journaling, which was printed on a clear transparency. Behind the transparency is a collection of chipboard letters that appear to be tumbling down the background. Look closely and you'll see "CTR" repeated in these letters.

Supplies: Cardstock; patterned paper (Hambly, Zsiage); chipboard letters (Fancy Pants, Zsiage); transparency (Hambly); acrylic paint; dictionary paper

Nicole Stark
Masters 2007

Sometimes, you can have too much of a good thing. In this instance, an oversupply of chipboard letters was used to create this flower embellishment. The cursive chipboard letters were first painted and then trimmed into bubbly petals. Next, the petals were arranged on top of patterned paper, which was trimmed to fit the flower shape. To finish, the flower center was filled with tiny buttons and brads.

Supplies: Patterned paper (Bo-Bunny, Daisy D's, Fancy Pants, Imagination Project); chipboard letters (Zsiage); dye ink; acrylic paint; brads; buttons (unknown); pen

Brooke Bartimioli
Masters 2007

Slide mounts are the perfect little frames, but there's got to be more to them than that!

Brooke Bartimioli
Masters 2007

Slide mounts can make super cool pockets on pages. On this layout, they house cute tags that explain the story of a stare-down between a cat and a bug. The slide mounts were backed with paper and then accented with stitched blocks of patterned paper. They were secured to the layout with three simple stitches (be sure the stitches allow room for the tag). Tags were inserted, and the layout was finished.

Supplies: Patterned paper (Daisy D's, encyclopedia pages, Fancy Pants, My Mind's Eye, Scenic Route, Wübie); slide mounts (unknown); letter stickers (Making Memories); rub-on accents (BasicGrey, Bo-Bunny, Making Memories); pigment ink; floss; twine; pen

Sometimes, even a mini album can seem too daunting. So, commitment phobes, this is the project for you! (Although, you might suffer some intimacy issues in regard to the personal topic—if you don't want to scrapbook about feelings, try a less intimidating topic, such as bowling.) Slide-mount albums are the minuets of mini albums. This album was created with the help of an adhesive-application machine: Run the mounts through the machine and apply patterned paper and photos. Bind the slide mounts with ribbon and embroidery floss.

Supplies: Slide mounts (Deluxe Designs); patterned paper (Urban Lily); paper flowers (Prima); glitter; ribbon (Michaels); floss (Making Memories); acrylic paint; foam adhesive; thread; pen

Michele Skinner
Masters 2007

We've definitely seen slide mounts used to frame smaller, support photos or to zero in on a detail in a larger photo. But never have we seen them used as photo corners. It's an easy technique to duplicate. Simply slide the mounts onto the corners of your photo and adhere to your page. This design was finished with a few additional slide mounts, which were used to frame small bits of patterned paper.

Supplies: Cardstock; slide mounts (Boxer); flowers, foam letters, patterned paper (AdornIt); chalk ink

Kelli Noto
Masters 2003

Of course, I use embroidery floss for stitching. What kinds of non-stitching inspiration can you give?

Ronee Parsons
Masters 2007

Embroidery floss deserves a little creative appreciation. Often, it only appears on scrapbook layouts as a walk-on role, providing a little stitching here and there. Finally, it is used as an integral part of design, and there is not a stitch to be seen. To create an understated and funky background, lines of embroidery floss were stretched across a piece of cardstock and then covered with clear gloss. Use your fingers to spread out the gloss. Once dry, you'll have a shiny, dimensional, striped background.

Supplies: Cardstock; patterned paper (Hambly); floss (DMC); labels (Dymo); dye ink; gel medium

I expected it to feel different...this grown up thing.

Most days, I don't feel like an adult.   I'm older, but not a   lot wiser.

I still get my feelings hurt & cry in my pillow.   I still listen to rock music really, really loud.

I still get   crushes on cute TV stars   {McDreamy anyone?}. I wish I   had recess.

I really wish that I had   naptime. My children   look to me for all the answers,

but I'm still figuring out   what the {important} questions are?

I have a little more   confidence than in my younger days.   I'm learning how

to say no.   I'm trying to stand up for myself.   I'm giving   myself permission

to leave the bed unmade & dishes in   the sink...and scrapbook instead.

I'm making time for   my friends...because grownups need playdates, too. So,

if being a grown up is supposed to be different   somehow {more serious?}

then I think I'll wait until I'm   40something...'cause right now

I'm digging being   30something.   {photo @ 35, journaling @ 36}

Wrap embroidery floss around a chipboard accent and have a page that is as touchable and cozy as a cable-knit sweater. This page was created on a background of paisleys. For dimension, a chipboard paisley was added. It was wrapped in embroidery floss to make it match the background. The floss was also wrapped around the chipboard number used in the title.

Supplies: Cardstock; patterned paper (We R Memory Keepers); chipboard letters (Heidi Swapp); floss (DMC); chipboard accent (Maya Road); felt flower (unknown); button

Katrina Simeck
Masters 2007

For pages about fashion, embroidery floss is a natural companion to the ribbon and fabric the artist used on this layout. Bright colors of floss, ribbon and fabric were chosen to match the equally bright colors of the shopping bags and photo subject's clothing. Little cross-stitches of pink floss pop up in all the right places on this layout, adding color and anchoring page elements.

Supplies: Cardstock; patterned paper (SEI); floss (DMC); transparent flower (Heidi Swapp); suede flower (Prima); flower brads (Provo Craft); flower ribbon (May Arts); notebook paper; tag (unknown); fabric; pen

Jeniece Higgins
Masters 2005

Totally tagged out. What are some ways to use lots of tags on one layout?

Crystal Jeffrey Rieger
Masters 2007

The tags on this background are reminiscent of tiny, white doghouses. Creating a background design with tags is an excellent way to use up excess. These tags were slightly unaligned on purpose (who wants to spend tons of time making sure all these darn things are straight?). Rub-on letters were applied across the design; the letters bridge the gaps of space between the tags, helping unify the look.

Supplies: Cardstock; tags (Avery); rub-on letters (American Crafts); rub-on accents (SEI); felt trim (Dollarama); staples

The beautiful patterns and colors of these randomly placed tags help them blend seamlessly together as a cool background for this page. Rhinestones were added to the tag centers to cover the holes and add a sparkle befitting of the photo subject. The journaling was printed onto green paper and cut into strips. At the same time, the green both contrasts and matches the background.

Supplies: Patterned paper, tags (BasicGrey); rhinestone brads (Karen Foster); chipboard letter (Pressed Petals); ribbon (Offray); letter stamps (Hero Arts); pigment ink

Shannon Taylor
Masters 2005

When is a tag not a tag? When it's grass, of course. You can turn colored tags into any sort of element with a little tearing and fringing of the edges. If your tags aren't the color you'd like them to be, paint them with layers of watercolor. First, crumble and then smooth out the tags for a little more texture. In addition to the tag grass, clear buttons are cleverly used to mimic the bubbles in this layout.

Supplies: Cardstock; patterned paper (A2Z Essentials, Hambly); tags; buttons (Buttons Galore) chipboard accents (Making Memories); chipboard letters (Pressed Petals); acrylic and watercolor paints; pen

Susan Cyrus
Masters 2004

What are some truly thematic ways to use fabric on pages?

Contrast is a wonderful way to spice up any design. When creating layouts, consider all the different ways to add contrast and then pick the most appropriate for your page theme, whether it be contrast in color, line quality or, in this case, texture. Shiny brads and lettering accents are juxtaposed with a funky fabric embellishment. See the instructions below to create this cute heart accent.

Supplies: Cardstock; patterned paper (Junkitz); transparency; bottle cap accents (Design Originals); crackle accent (Ranger); alcohol and dye inks; color wash, embossing ink and powder, metallic mixatives, ultra thick embossing enamel (Ranger); chipboard letters (Li'l Davis); letter stamps (Hero Arts); word stamp (Posh Impressions); rub-on accents (Making Memories, Rusty Pickle); tag (Avery); white cotton fabric; melting pot; non-stick craft sheet

Lisa Dixon
Masters 2004

HOW'D SHE DO THAT?

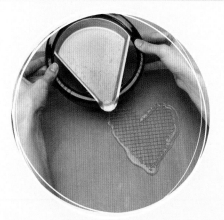

1 Cut a heart from a small square of metallic utility cloth (this can be purchased in the gardening department of your local hardware store). Melt extra-thick embossing enamel and line the perimeter of the heart, covering any sharp edges.

2 Color the cooled embossing powder with alcohol inks applied with an ink applicator or any soft cloth.

3 Weave torn lengths of cotton fabric (these were hand-dyed) through the holes in the utility cloth. Trim the ends and adhere to page with heavy-duty, double-sided tape.

A hug. Often the only barrier between the two people sharing the embrace is simple fabric. The fabric on this page symbolizes a big, grandpa hug, and it comes from the very telltale blue shirts once worn by a cherished patriarch. Fabric was trimmed from the shirt to encase a 12" x 12" (30cm x 30cm) block of chipboard. After the fabric was stretched, it was adhered to the chipboard with double-sided tape. The title letters were also cut from the collection and sewn to the layout for added depth. The journaling explains the story of the blue shirts for a granddaughter who never had the honor of knowing her grandpa.

Supplies: Cardstock; shirt fabric (from personal collection); sandpaper; lined paper; staples; thread; pen

Catherine Feegel-Erhardt
Masters 2007

What once was painted a minty shade of toothpaste green, (not by our choice – but by the previous owners!)… Has now been transformed into one of my favorite spaces in the entire house. Warm, caramel colored walls, a shiny, vaulted wood-paneled ceiling, lots of natural light, comfy lived-in leather furniture, felt décor pillows found on clearance at Target(!), tons of orange accents, and the perfect Pottery Barn lamp… All complete the look of our much-loved and often-used…

COZY

SunRoom

With all of the wonderful patterned fabrics available, it's easy to overlook plain fabric as a wonderful blank canvas. Try stamping on fabric for a completely custom look. On this layout, cotton fabric in warm colors was stamped with solvent-based ink. More flowers were cut from felt to add texture. Buttons were sewn to the middle of the flowers for pops of color and dimension.

Susan Weinroth
Masters 2006

Supplies: Cardstock; buttons, brads, felt flowers, ribbon, letter stickers (American Crafts); letter tabs (Scrapworks); solvent ink; felt; floss; cotton fabric; Florida-TS font (My Fonts)

I am plum out of ideas for using my flower stash. Please help!

This project proves that the phrase "love letters" is open to interpretation. These decorated letters feature sweet flowers, each used in a different way. On the first, a single flower accents a tied length of black ribbon, helping hide the knot. The second letter is completely engulfed in flower love. A flower is sandwiched inside a glass frame on the third, and the fourth letter is graced with a simple column of flowers.

Supplies: Wooden letters, patterned paper (Creative Imaginations); cardstock; ribbon (Offray); brad, large silk flower, rub-on accent (Hot Off The Press); small flowers (unknown); metal word accent (Westrim); metal frame accent (unknown)

Samantha Walker
Masters 2005

Little girls in flowered sweaters are just irresistible; the inspiration for using flowers on this page came from the felt flowers sewn on the photo subject's clothing. To create the focal point, a flower was handcut from purple felt and then surrounded with smaller flowers also handcut from felt in coordinating colors. The bright colors of the flowers and corresponding background paper match the exuberant feeling of the photo.

Katrina Simeck
Masters 2007

Supplies: Cardstock; patterned paper (One Heart One Mind); chipboard letters (Zsiage); felt flowers, rub-on letters (American Crafts); dimensional adhesive; brads; button; thread

Photo: Bryan Farley;
Brooks Institute of Photography

Flowers are such a huge part of weddings, symbolizing the blooming love of two people, that their absence on a wedding layout would be strange. Lovely little paper flowers were used to frame three gorgeous photos on this layout, imparting the look of a bride's bouquet. Choosing to use ivory flowers maintains a delicate sophistication that does not distract from the photos.

Supplies: Cardstock; patterned paper (K&Co.); flowers (7gypsies, EK Success, Jo-Ann's, Making Memories, My Mind's Eye); pearl studs, rhinestones (Making Memories); chipboard accent (Fancy Pants); acrylic paint; circle cutter; corner rounder; thread; transparency

Perfection is perhaps the best way to sum up this special day. I worried for months about the decision to have an outdoor wedding and just kept my fingers crossed it wouldn't be too hot or rain on everything. Now, an apple orchard may be considered a somewhat unorthodox location for a ceremony, but my grandmother's garden was a perfect site on my family's farm. It all came together beautifully. Looking back I just remember it was a wonderfully perfect day.

Lisa Tutman-Oglesby
Masters 2007

I have tons of ribbon scraps—what are some cute ways to use them?

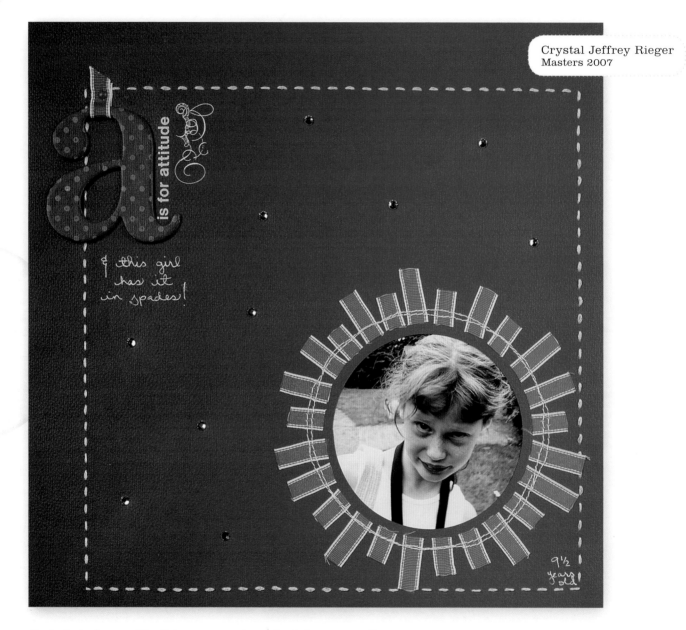

Crystal Jeffrey Rieger
Masters 2007

Cool photo frames like this are a great use for leftover bits of ribbon. To start, cut a frame window from the background paper and cut ribbon into varying lengths. Ribbon lengths can be adhered in a variety of ways, such as with staples, but here they were stitched to the page background (secure ribbon with a small amount of tacky adhesive first). Once the ribbon is adhered and stitched, add the photo face-up to the back of the layout so it shows through the frame. This is a wonderful starburst frame, but also try the technique with square and rectangle frames. Add more spice with ribbon lengths in a variety of colors and patterns.

Supplies: Cardstock; ribbon (Michaels); rub-on letters (ChartPak); brad; chipboard letter, rub-on accent (BasicGrey); floss; thread; rhinestones; acrylic paint; stamp (Technique Tuesday); pigment ink; pen

Ribbons are definitely the unifying factor on this layout—their consistent use to accent almost every element really ties the page together. The playful mix of ribbon patterns adds spunk and was successful because they come from a coordinating set. First, the chipboard heart was wrapped with bits of ribbon. The photo was complemented with ribbon as well; a chipboard embellishment was tied to pink grosgrain ribbon and then the entire accent was stapled to the page background.

Diana Graham
Masters 2003

Supplies: Cardstock; chipboard accents, patterned paper, ribbon (KI Memories); large chipboard heart, chipboard letter (Fancy Pants); rhinestone word (Heidi Swapp); transparent overlay (My Mind's Eye); rhinestone accent (Hobby Lobby); journaling square (Reminisce); glitter; cartoon accent (Internet download); corner rounder; sandpaper; stamping ink; pen

Ribbon is an apt embellishment for pages that express warmth, comfort and joy. A dimensional harlequin pattern was created with ribbon and chipboard (again, a great technique for your leftover stash) for this page about a dearly loved grandma. Begin by trimming lengths of ribbon and organize into groups. Working with one piece of chipboard at a time, cover with spray adhesive and apply ribbon. Once the adhesive is dry, trim around the edges of the chipboard. Accent the centers of silk flowers by using a die-cutting machine to cut small circles of ribbon and secure to the centers with mini brads. When trimming and cutting shapes from ribbon, rub some clear-drying glue on the edges to prevent fraying.

Supplies: Patterned paper (Daisy D's); ribbon (Bazzill, Making Memories, Offray, SEI); buttons (Autumn Leaves); flowers (Prima); brads; chipboard shapes (Fancy Pants); flower centers, photo corner (QuicKutz); rub-on word, tags (Making Memories); pen

Nicole Stark
Masters 2007

THE NEW
frontier

"Reuse. Repurpose. Recycle."

This eco-friendly mantra can also be applied to your scrapbooking skills. Your entire life deserves a creative touch, and as you explore the following pages, you will see that anything (such as items from the junk drawer, stuff designated for the trash pile and things cluttering up your closets) can be transformed into memory art.

It may seem scary, but it's time to step outside the layout. Non-scrapbooking surfaces exist in strange, new sizes or shapes. Or worse! These surfaces may not even be FLAT like a trusty scrapbook page. But think of it as putting the "U" in utility. And, let's face it: It's cheaper than redecorating. All of these cool little projects will add life and love to your walls, allowing you to change the look and style of your nooks and crannies very inexpensively. If you are experiencing creative block, these projects will zap you with energy. They will force you into a new zone with the potential to unlock hidden artistic genius.

What are a few ways to spice up my accordion albums?

Nicole Stark
Masters 2007

What could be a more perfect home for a single day's worth of photos than a mini album? This mini album was handcrafted to perfection to house beautiful fall photos. To create a similar album, cover two blocks of chipboard with cardstock; these will be the front and back of the album. Then, create the layouts you intend to use. For consistency and design unity, choose a collection of accents that can be carried throughout the entire album. For example, the tags, journaling stamp, transparency and mesh accents appear throughout the entirety of this album. Once the pages are finished, assemble them into the album so that alternate folds are created.

Supplies: Patterned paper (BasicGrey, dictionary pages, KI Memories); transparency (Hambly, My Mind's Eye); sticker accents (7gypsies); button, mini tags, rub-on accents, word sticker (Making Memories); chipboard accent (Fancy Pants); manila tags (Avery); mesh (Magic Mesh); acrylic paint, photo corners, transparent letters (Heidi Swapp); ribbon (Offray); brads; pigment ink; journaling stamp (Autumn Leaves); staples; pen

Vanessa Hudson
Masters 2006

Mini albums are compact expressions of love, but sometimes they can leave a scrapbooker wanting more—more space, that is. Accordion-folded elements are an easy way to accommodate extra photos, journaling and other accents. To lessen any extra bulk the accordion album might cause, a square was cut from the chipboard page of the mini album, thereby making the fold-out element flush with the album.

Supplies: Chipboard album (Maya Road); patterned paper (BasicGrey); transparency (Hambly); brads, photo turns (Junkitz); heart clip, rub-on accents (Making Memories); stamp (Autumn Leaves); tag (unknown); felt hearts, ribbon (American Craft); acrylic paint; buttons; floss; pen

ompleting a large-format scrapbook album can intimidate even the most seasoned veteran. Accordion albums are a wonderful alternative, especially for scrapbook-essay projects. Scrapbook essays require only a few layouts and have a central focus. This album captures Catherine's family, just as they are, in the year 2007. The photos and the journaling support that theme. She created a page for each member, picking patterns, colors and accents that convey the person's energy and personality. The pages show that, despite all their differences, they are a strong family unit.

Supplies: Cardstock; patterned paper (A2Z Essentials, American Crafts, BasicGrey, Chatterbox, Heidi Swapp, Reminisce, Robin's Nest); transparency (Hambly); rub-ons (American Crafts, Heidi Swapp, Making Memories); ribbons (American Crafts, May Arts, Michaels, Strano); flower (Heidi Swapp); charms; staples; brads; eyelets; stamping ink; bookplates (Heidi Swapp, Making Memories); acrylic paint; sandpaper; tags (Making Memories); thread

Catherine Feegel-Erhardt
Masters 2007

Are board book projects really that involved?

Jeniece Higgins
Masters 2005

This board book project looks deceptively complex, but in reality, it qualifies as quick and easy. The collection of bright and beautiful patterned papers hails from a theme pack of papers, so it was a cinch to mix and match them. Embellishments were kept to a minimum to lessen the bulkiness of the project and to keep the focus on the photos. The papers and embellishments were sanded and inked to add dimension and texture.

Supplies: Board book, burlap ribbon (unknown); accents, borders, patterned paper (Dèjá Views); flowers (Prima); brads; decoupage medium; stamping inks; pen

Board book projects have "family fun time" written all over them. For this project, Jill's children were given the honor of chalking the pages. The result is a heartfelt project and a room full of smiling faces. The front and back covers of this book were spray painted with chalkboard paint, which you can find at your local hardware store. Hairspray was used to seal the actual chalkings on the inside of the album.

Supplies: Board book (Maya Road); fibers, patterned paper (BasicGrey); transparencies (Creative Imaginations, Hambly); tags (7gypsies); epoxy stickers (unknown); chalkboard paint (Home Depot); hairspray; glossy sealer; chalk; pen

Jill Jackson-Mills
Masters 2007

If repurposing a children's board book, which can be found at any bookstore or even at thrift stores, seems daunting, scrapbook companies now manufacture board books that require little prep time to use.

They also are available in a variety of sizes, which means you can get your feet wet by creating a smaller project.

This board book was decorated with coordinating patterned papers and embellishments, ensuring everything matches perfectly.

Supplies: Board book (K&Co.); cardstock; chipboard hearts and letters, fibers, letter stickers, patterned paper, rub-on accents (BasicGrey); rhinestones (Heidi Swapp); die-cut hearts (QuickKutz); definition stickers (Creative Imaginations, Making Memories); photo corner (Colorbök); stamping ink; thread; dried berries; pen

Lisa Tutman-Oglesby
Masters 2007

I'm tired of store-bought calendars and would like some ideas for making my own.

Your daily planner deserves some of your creativity. It is, after all, something you spend time with every day to help manage your busy life. Find coordinating patterned paper in a style indicative to you and adhere it to the front and back covers. On this planner, Katrina ran a ribbon across the front with an important daily reminder: "Find balance." Ribbon is also used to gussy up the spiral binding.

Supplies: Planner (Per Annum); cardstock; die-cut arrow, patterned paper, sticker accents (Scenic Route); chipboard letters (Zsiage); rub-on accent (One Heart One Mind); ribbon (American Crafts, Offray)

Katrina Simeck
Masters 2007

Dry-erase calendars are awesome because they give you the opportunity to wipe the slate clean every month, which can be a mentally cleansing ritual. Repositionable adhesive is the secret to this board. The letter stickers, which act as great at-a-glance reminders for birthdays and other occasions, are easy to remove, and the tags were adhered with temporary adhesive. Remove these babies at the end of each month to make way for new ones. Dry-erase markers fill in the rest of the details.

Crystal Jeffrey Rieger
Masters 2007

Supplies: Board (Board Dudes); die-cut letters, fibers, letter stickers, patterned paper, tags (BasicGrey); corner rounder; dry erase marker; pen

Creative calendars are a natural project for scrapbookers. As a scrapbooker, you are already super in tune to the details of life; your custom calendar will give you daily inspiration. This calendar is 8" x 8" (20cm x 20cm), a good format to use because 8" x 8" papers are readily available. Designing the calendar was easy—once the photo and calendar page were placed, it was just a matter of adding elements in a balanced and eye-pleasing manner.

Supplies: Chipboard; cardstock; patterned paper (Scenic Route); letter stickers (Heidi Swapp, Scenic Route); calendar (printout from computer); die-cut shapes (Deluxe Designs); sequin bracket (Queen & Co.); ribbon (Cactus Pink); buttons (Autumn Leaves); book rings; latex paint; hole punch; pen

Nic Howard
Masters 2005

HOW'D SHE DO THAT?

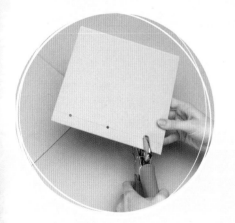

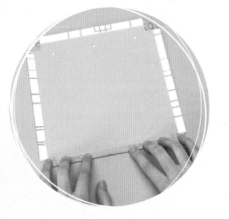

1 Cut two pieces of chipboard to 8" x 8" (20cm x 20cm). With a pencil, draw a line 1½" (4cm) in from one side. Punch three equally-spaced holes along this line. Repeat with the second piece of chipboard.

2 Cut two pieces of patterned paper to 9" x 9" (23cm x 23cm). Center one piece of chipboard onto a piece of paper. First fold the corners over the chipboard and glue, then fold and glue each of the four sides. Repunch the holes. Repeat with the other pieces of chipboard and paper.

3 Cut two pieces of patterned paper to 7¾" x 7¾" (19cm x 19cm). Glue these to the inside of the chipboard pieces. Repunch the holes. Create pages for the calendar, punching holes in each.

Show me some cool ways to gussy up wooden monograms.

Lisa Tutman-Oglesby
Masters 2007

This beautiful message is the perfect inspiration for any scrapbooker's creative nook. Purchase plain wooden letters, gather a mix of patterned paper to complement your scrapbook décor, and paint to match. Once the paint is dry, trace the letters onto the back of the patterned papers. Trim letters from papers and apply to the letters, making sure to smooth any wrinkles. Use a craft knife to trim jagged or overhanging edges.

Supplies: Wooden letters (unknown); chipboard accents, patterned paper, rub-on accents (Heidi Grace); acrylic paint; chalk

Monogram letters don't always have to signify the first letter of someone's name; they can be used to honor a hobby or favorite sport. This letter shows a love of soccer. Harlequin patterned paper was used to mimic the black-and-white design of a soccer ball. Ribbons also add thematic punch while a few soccer ball accents finish the design. Finally the letter was adhered to the acrylic frame.

Supplies: Acrylic frame; wooden letter (unknown); patterned paper (Bo-Bunny); letter stickers (Heidi Swapp); soccer accents (EK Success); ribbon (Creative Imaginations, Offray); chain (Leisure Arts); decoupage medium; paint; stamping ink

Kathy Fesmire
Masters 2004

Catherine Feegel-Erhardt
Masters 2007

Hanging monogram letters on the walls of your home is very trendy these days. The letters can be found at home-décor stores, but they can be expensive and are generally plain. Your local hobby store will carry inexpensive craft letters. This letter was created for a lovely daughter. Mom mixed the paints to match the patterned paper she used to cover the letter. The edges of the letter were inked and a flourish was stamped along the stem of the letter. Jewels were added to the photo tag for girly bling. Transparent plastic letters and a halved silk flower were inked for dimension.

Supplies: Wooden letter (Darice); flower, patterned paper, sparkle accents, transparent letters (Heidi Swapp); ribbons (Making Memories, May Arts); stamp (Autumn Leaves); tag (Making Memories); acrylic paint; foam adhesive

I have an old clipboard lying around—what are some creative ways to use it?

Ronee Parsons
Masters 2007

If you have an old clipboard lying around the house, give it a new life—turn it into an artsy photo frame. Ronee likes the look of hand-tied books, which is where the knotted-ribbon idea comes from. Lengths of self-adhesive ribbon were wrapped around the board and knotted together. The adhesive made the ribbon easy to apply and ensures its security (ribbon can stretch and fall off the board without proper adhesive). An adorable photo with rounded corners (notice how they match the rounded corners of the clipboard) was placed on top and anchored with a chipboard letter.

Supplies: Clipboard (unknown); cardstock; ribbon (Fancy Pants, SEI, Shoebox Trims); adhesive ribbon (Die Cuts With A View); chipboard (Fancy Pants); corner rounder

Keep the romance alive in your life with this idea: a clipboard dedicated to love notes. Decorate the background much like you would a scrapbook page. This one looks great with the pattern-blocked design and endearing photo of the happy couple. Chipboard accents and tags finish the project.

Supplies: Clipboard (unknown); cardstock; chipboard letter, die-cut hearts, patterned paper, rub-on accents (BasicGrey); photo corner (One Heart One Mind); ribbon (SEI)

now and forever

u & me

LOVE

notes

Katrina Simeck
Masters 2007

School ROCKS

Mrs. Jennings

Back 2school

Teachers, like parents, can be underappreciated. Show your child's teacher you care with a personalized clipboard. The receiving teacher will no doubt be touched by the gesture. Tons of school-themed papers and accents exist (you probably already have some in your scrap stash) to help make your own clipboard totally special.

Kellie Noto
Masters 2003

Supplies: Clipboard (unknown); circle and star accents, patterned paper (AdornIt); ribbon (AdornIt, Jo-Ann's); die-cut letters (QuicKutz); chalk ink

I'm thinking about accenting a frame with leftover supplies. How should I go about it?

Susan Cyrus
Masters 2004

Photo: Marissa Bowers

Inspiration for this frame came from the stickers that were used. They were packaged so cleverly, in a design similar to the one on the frame. Susan simply mimicked it. Place the large stickers first; try to place them so they somewhat balance the frame; you certainly don't want to be too perfect. Then, work with the next largest stickers and so on until your frame is covered.

Supplies: Frame (unknown); letter and number stickers (Making Memories); decoupage medium

This is a quick project that would make a fantastic and heartfelt gift. Frames are inexpensive and easy to find at most department stores. This one features a multi-photo layout; such layouts will look best if your photos show some kind of unity. For example, these are all of the same subject, close-up in perspective and were printed in black and white. Rub-ons and a tag add some color to the otherwise white background.

Supplies: Frame (Target); epoxy stickers, letter stickers (Creative Imaginations); cardstock sticker (Paper Loft); tag (BasicGrey); ribbon (Michaels)

Michele Skinner
Masters 2007

We could all use an inspirational reminder like this on our walls. How cool is this frame? The fact that it's super easy to create makes it even cooler. Take a light-colored wooden frame and remove the glass and backing. Grab some stickers and adhere them to the frame to use as masks. Take some dark brown ink, pour it directly on the frame and wipe it with a paper towel to completely saturate the wood (rub with the grain of the wood). Once it's dry, remove the stickers. Use stamps and rub-ons to print an inspirational quote onto a transparency. Place eyelets in the corners of the transparency and tie to the frame with twine.

Supplies: Frame; letter stickers (Arctic Frog, BasicGrey, SEI); stamps (Paper Salon, Purple Onion); transparency; rub-on letters (Fancy Pants); eyelets; twine; dye ink

Ronee Parsons
Masters 2007

I've got some spare glass jars just lying around. What can I do with them?

Covering a jar with fabric can seem tricky, but it will actually produce better results than paper. Fabric has much more give than paper, allowing it to bend and flex with the curves of the jar. Cut enough fabric to tuck inside the jar. Insert floral foam snuggly into the jar so it secures the fabric. Create double-sided flowers from patterned paper (cut two flower shapes per flower). Cover the wrong side of the paper flowers with decoupage medium, slip wire between the flowers and press together. Tie tulle leaves around the wire stems and insert the stems into the floral foam.

Supplies: Glass jar; patterned paper (Cloud 9, Heidi Grace, KI Memories); buttons, fabric, floral foam, floral paper stems (Jo-Ann's); tulle (Target); decoupage medium; gift tag (Hallmark)

Jill Jackson-Mills
Masters 2007

7 lbs. 9 oz.

20 ½ Inches

Lillian

Grace

Bourgeault

July 14, 2004

4:33 pm

Canning jars can be as beautiful as they are useful. Painted or left as is, they can be transformed from food storage to flower display. These paper flowers will live forever inside this jar as will the image of this adorable newborn. Paint the jar with thick coats of acrylic paint. Create flowers from patterned paper and wooden dowels. Set the flowers into floral foam inside the jar and enjoy.

Supplies: Glass jar; acrylic paint; patterned paper (Chatterbox); letter stickers (American Crafts); wooden dowels; circle punches; floral foam; bumble bee accent (Petaloo)

Jennifer Bourgeault
Masters 2004

This jar full of candy, once looked just of glass, sure became dandy when treated with some creative sass. This project could be completed in a few hours, and it also is a good way to use supply scraps. Trim strips of patterned paper to cover the circumference of the jar. Add ribbon and mesh. Cover the top with a circle of patterned paper and add a silk flower and chipboard.

Denise Tucker
Masters 2004

Supplies: Glass jar; chipboard letters, patterned paper (Rusty Pickle); mesh (Magic Mesh); ribbon (BasicGrey); flowers (Teters); jumbo brad (Bazzill); stamping ink (BasicGrey); rhinestones (Heidi Swapp); die-cut hearts (QuicKutz); definition stickers (Creative Imaginations, Making Memories); photo corner (Colorbök); stamping ink; thread; dried berries; pen

Discarded CDs seem full of creative potential. Any ideas?

Crystal Jeffrey Rieger
Masters 2007

Using a CD as a creative surface can give surprisingly good results. The surface area is just the right size to house one photo and some journaling, which makes for easy projects. The material is also sturdy, so you can add bulkier embellishments without worry of bent pages. To create a CD album like this one, paint CDs with acrylic paint and let dry. Create the paper pages using coordinating patterned paper, stickers and other embellishments. Adhere ribbon to the CD surface and then add the pages. This project can be an album, or you can use it as a wall hanging.

Supplies: CD (IBM); patterned paper, ribbon, accent and letter stickers (SEI); acrylic paint; pen

CDs that would otherwise be discarded (for example, all of the free-trial CDs that Internet Service providers send out) can be made into very creative gift tags. This one was created for a daughter celebrating her sweet 16th birthday. Both sides were covered with patterned paper and the edges were inked. A bright pink silk flower rests on one side. The other side holds the keys and the message, which was spelled with letter stickers and chipboard numbers.

Supplies: CD; patterned paper (My Mind's Eye); chipboard letters (EK Success); stamps (Creative Imaginations); rub-on accents (Old Time Pottery); letter stickers (Miss Elizabeth's); ribbon (Offray); decoupage medium; chain (Leisure Arts); keys

Kathy Fesmire
Masters 2004

Valerie Barton
Masters 2003

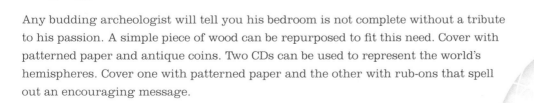

Any budding archeologist will tell you his bedroom is not complete without a tribute to his passion. A simple piece of wood can be repurposed to fit this need. Cover with patterned paper and antique coins. Two CDs can be used to represent the world's hemispheres. Cover one with patterned paper and the other with rub-ons that spell out an encouraging message.

Supplies: Patterned paper (Crate Paper, Flair Designs); CDs; Scrabble™ letter stickers (EK Success); antique coins (Karen Foster); rub-on accents (Making Memories); wood; paint; handle; rope; key

Every week I throw away the cutest little mint tins, and it seems like such a waste. What can I do with them?

Curiously strong design options, that's what tins from a certain brand of mints offer. (Altoids, anyone? Go on, take two; it's the recommended dosage.) This project was created in honor of the almighty Apple iPod® because the mint tin and audio player are approximately the same size. The tin opens into an accordion album that lists the iPod owner's favorite songs.

Supplies: Accordion book, mint tin (Pinecone Press); cardstock; patterned paper (Urban Lily); rub-on letters (American Crafts); flowers (Prima); rhinestones (Heidi Swapp); ribbon (unknown); stamps (Autumn Leaves)

Katrina Simeck
Masters 2007

This project would be well suited for any mom-to-be or for a cherished friend expecting a baby. What once housed mints now contains adorable cards. The custom-created cards in this tin were left blank so family members and friends could compose sweet messages to the newborn, but you could also create cards for the purpose of capturing the birth story, significance of the baby's name, birth chart as well as the birthing stats, such as weight and length. This tin was sanded and then painted with two coats of blue. Lots of crackle medium was then applied and, once dry, silver paint was brushed on top. Magnetic words were inked and added to the top. The tiny sign was anchored with a sewing bobbin.

Supplies: Mint tin; patterned paper (Daisy D's, My Mind's Eye); letter stickers (Making Memories); word magnets (Magnetic Poetry); clock (7gypsies); labels (Dymo); rub-on accents (Daisy D's, Karen Foster); sticker accents (Acrtic Frog); acrylic paint; crackle medium; stamping ink; sewing bobbin; wire; buttons; pen

Brooke Bartimioli
Masters 2007

I have a credenza full of these round tins. Surely, they can be put to good use?

Michele Skinner
Masters 2007

Around the holidays, these round metal tins seem to multiply in our homes like rabbits. Repurpose these tins like so and your cake will be the prettiest of the potluck. Paint a base coat of paint all over the tin (lightly sand the surface of the tin for a smooth paint application). Use decoupage medium to adhere patterned paper around the tin; carefully smooth out any wrinkles. Finish with chipboard letters, paper flowers and trim.

Supplies: Tin with lid (Williams-Sonoma); paper trim, patterned paper (Doodlebug); paper flowers (Prima); chipboard letters (Scenic Route); liquid pearls; acrylic paint; decoupage medium; cake decorating accessories

This compact mini album is so compact that it fits on a Christmas tree without over-burdening the branch from which it hangs. Each year, Jessie creates an ornament inspired from a family memory. This year, Disneyland beat out the other wonderful Baldwin family memories, and a round tin was a natural choice for creating a mouse head. Photos were adhered back-to-back to a length of ribbon and placed inside.

Supplies: Round tin (unknown); cardstock; spiral clip (Making Memories); ribbon (Michaels); circle punch; pen

Jessie Baldwin
Masters 2005

All of the colorful beads on this tin make it look like a yummy, sprinkle-topped cupcake. But it actually was created to hold all of the stuff of a boy's life—the tiny stuff at least. This project is easy, but it requires the patience of only completing a section at a time. Apply clear-drying, tacky craft glue to a quarter of the surface and sprinkle with beads. Stabilize the tin so it doesn't roll and allow to dry before completing the remaining sections.

Supplies: Tin (Michaels); beads (Wal-Mart); diamond glaze (JudiKins); patterned paper (My Mind's Eye); rub-on letters (American Crafts); arrow accents (EK Success)

Shannon Taylor
Masters 2005

I love using lunch boxes as scrapbook albums, and I want even more ideas.

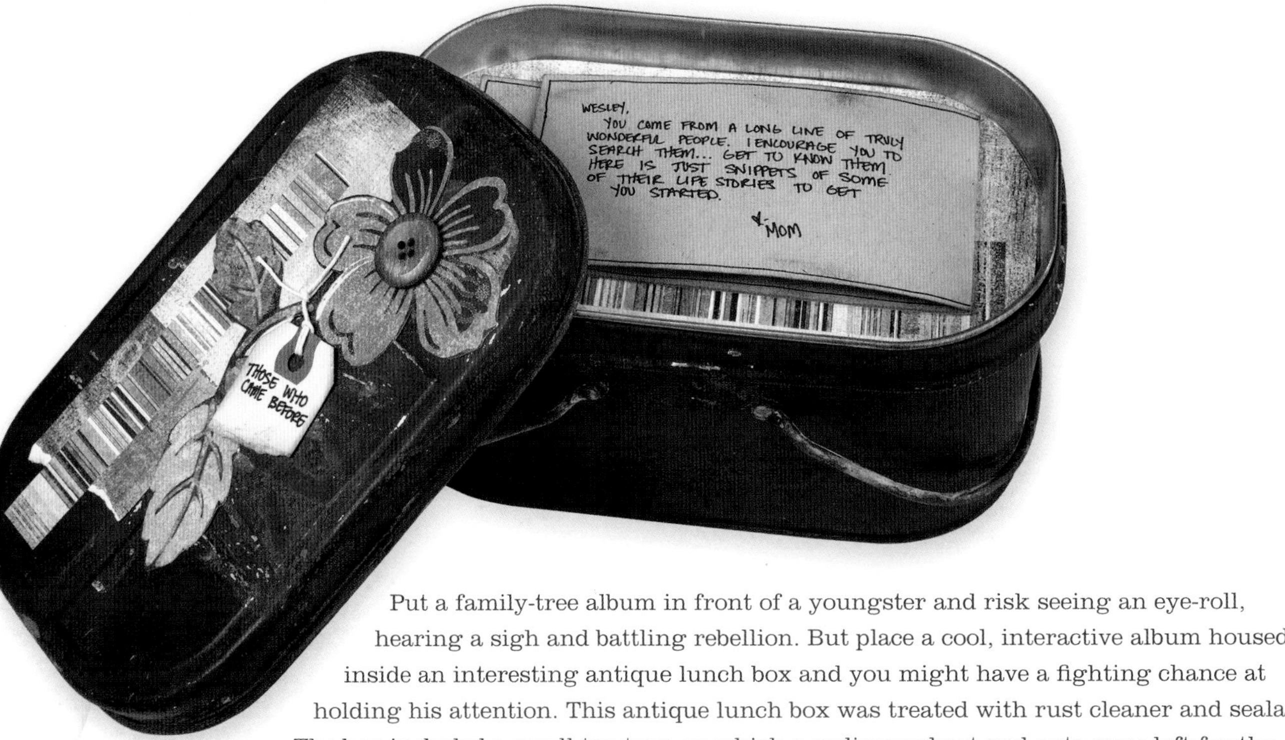

WESLEY,
YOU CAME FROM A LONG LINE OF TRULY WONDERFUL PEOPLE. I ENCOURAGE YOU TO SEARCH THEM... GET TO KNOW THEM. HERE IS JUST SNIPPETS OF SOME OF THEIR LIFE STORIES TO GET YOU STARTED.
♥ MOM
THOSE WHO CAME BEFORE

Put a family-tree album in front of a youngster and risk seeing an eye-roll, hearing a sigh and battling rebellion. But place a cool, interactive album housed inside an interesting antique lunch box and you might have a fighting chance at holding his attention. This antique lunch box was treated with rust cleaner and sealant. The box included a small top tray on which a pedigree chart and note were left for the recipient. The album inside was modeled after a rolodex and made with a chipboard base bound to pages with elastic cording. It can be easily removed and replaced.

Supplies: Metal tin (unknown); cardstock; patterned paper (BasicGrey); buttons (Autumn Leaves); tags (Avery); dye and pigment ink; beading elastic (Stretch-Rite); pen

THOSE WHO CAME BEFORE
DAVID E. & SARAH MINERVA CHARD

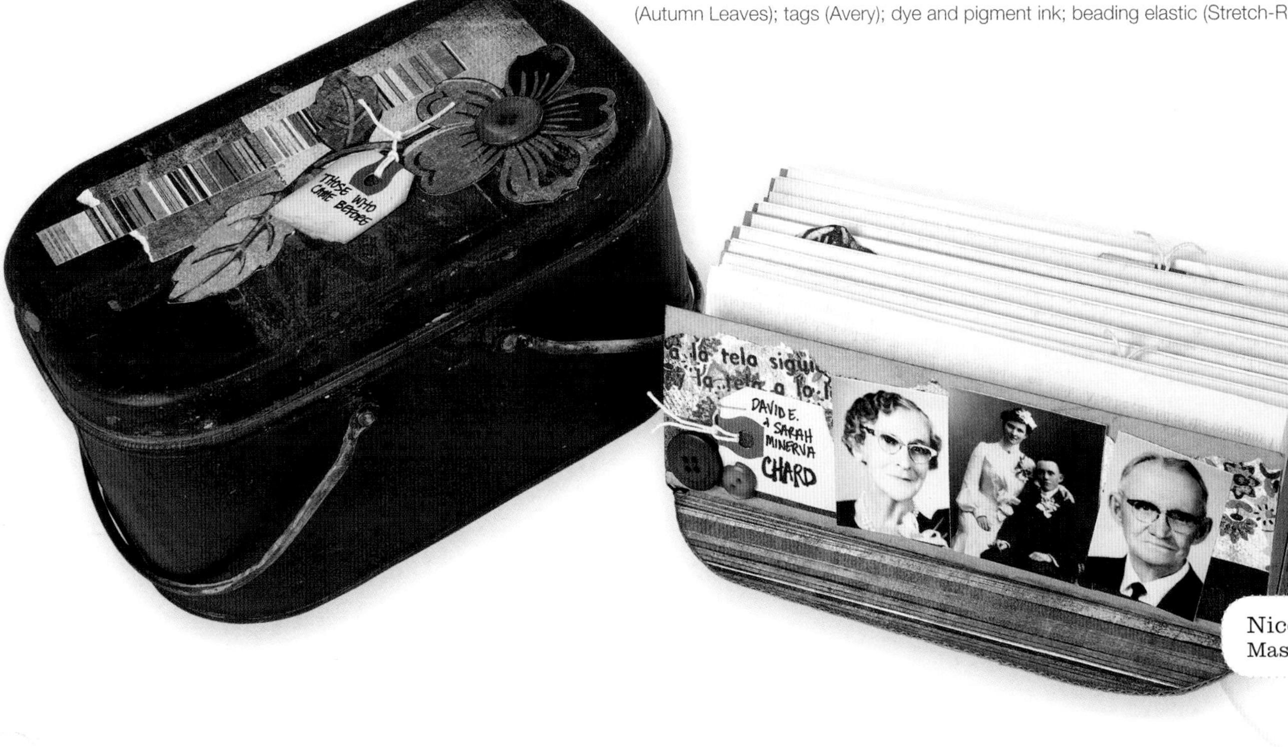

Nicole Stark
Masters 2007

A tisket, a tasket, what great recipes will fill this lunch-pail basket! Torrey is a sucker for texture, so this dainty pail is full of it. What looks like patterned paper is actually created from a mix of paint, clear glaze and a healthy amount of modeling paste. Mix these three ingredients to desired texture and color and apply to the pail. Press brass flower stencils into the mix for embossed designs. Line the rim of the top with a pleated strip of paper and ribbon.

Create the recipe cards from paper and label tape.

Torrey Scott
Masters 2003

Supplies: Papier-mâché pail (Michaels); patterned paper (Karen Foster, KI Memories, Paper Studio); glazing medium, modeling paste (Golden); gel paint; acrylic paint; stencil (Delta); ribbon (Offray); label maker (Dymo)

We journalers need a safe place to store our thoughts. This brightly decorated lunchbox is the perfect home. Cut patterned paper to fit the pail and add matching ribbon and punched paper accents for flair. Paper and silk flowers accented with buttons, brads and rhinestones bloom around the corner of the pail and across the top. Chipboard letters in a fun collection of colors and sealed with finishing coat add the final touch.

Supplies: Lunch box (Hobby Lobby); patterned paper, ribbon (American Crafts); chipboard letters (Heidi Swapp); paper flowers (Prima); silk flowers (Teters); solid buttons (Wal-Mart); fabric brads, printed button (Paper Studio); confetti flowers (Queen & Co.); rhinestones (Crafts Etc.); magnet accent (Big Lots); decoupage medium; Crop-a-Dile eyelet tool (We R Memory Keepers)

Kathy Fesmire
Masters 2004

source guide

The following companies manufacture products featured in this book. Please check your local retailers to find these materials, or go to a company's Web site for the latest product. In addition, we have made every attempt to properly credit the items mentioned in this book. We apologize to any company that we have listed incorrectly, and we would appreciate hearing from you.

3L Corporation
(800) 828-3130
www.scrapbook-adhesives.com

3M
(800) 364-3577
www.3m.com

7gypsies
(877) 749-7797
www.sevengypsies.com

A2Z Essentials
(419) 663-2869
www.geta2z.com

Adobe Systems Incorporated
(800) 833-6687
www.adobe.com

Adornit/Carolee's Creations
(435) 563-1100
www.adornit.com

Aleene's — see Duncan Enterprises

American Crafts
(801) 226-0747
www.americancrafts.com

American Traditional Designs
(800) 448-6656
www.americantraditional.com

ANW Crestwood
(973) 406-5000
www.anwcrestwood.com

Arctic Frog
(479) 636-3764
www.arcticfrog.com

Around The Block
(801) 593-1946
www.aroundtheblockproducts.com

Autumn Leaves
(800) 588-6707
www.autumnleaves.com

Avery Dennison Corporation
(800) 462-8379
www.avery.com

BasicGrey
(801) 544-1116
www.basicgrey.com

Bazzill Basics Paper
(480) 558-8557
www.bazzillbasics.com

Berwick Offray, LLC
(800) 344-5533
www.offray.com

Big Lots
www.biglots.com

Board Dudes, Inc.
(951) 808-9347
www.boarddudes.com

Bo-Bunny Press
(801) 771-4010
www.bobunny.com

Boxer Scrapbook Productions, LLC
(888) 625-6255
www.boxerscrapbooks.com

Buttons Galore & More
(856) 753-6700
www.buttonsgaloreandmore.com

Cactus Pink
(866) 798-2446
www.cactuspink.com

ChartPak
(800) 628-1910
www.chartpak.com

Chatterbox, Inc.
(888) 416-6260
www.chatterboxinc.com

Cloud 9 Design
(866) 348-5661
www.cloud9design.biz

Collage Press
(435) 676-2039
www.collagepress.com

Colorbök, Inc.
(800) 366-4660
www.colorbok.com

Cosmo Cricket
(800) 852-8810
www.cosmocricket.com

Crafter's Workshop, The
(877) 272-3837
www.thecraftersworkshop.com

Crafts, Etc. Ltd.
(800) 888-0321 x 1275
www.craftsetc.com

Crate Paper
(801) 798-8996
www.cratepaper.com

Creative Imaginations
(800) 942-6487
www.cigift.com

Creative Impressions
(719) 596-4860
www.creativeimpressions.com

Creative Memories
(800) 468-9335
www.creativememories.com

Dafont
www.dafont.com

Daisy Bucket Designs
(541) 289-3299
www.daisybucketdesigns.com

Daisy D's Paper Company
(888) 601-8955
www.daisydspaper.com

Darice, Inc.
(800) 321-1494
www.darice.com

Dèjá Views
(800) 243-8419
www.dejaviews.com

Delta Technical Coatings, Inc.
(800) 423-4135
www.deltacrafts.com

Deluxe Designs
(480) 497-9005
www.deluxecuts.com

Design Originals
(800) 877-0067
www.d-originals.com

Die Cuts With A View
(801) 224-6766
www.diecutswithaview.com

DMC Corp.
(973) 589-0606
www.dmc-usa.com

Dollarama
www.dollarama.com

Doodlebug Design Inc.
(877) 800-9190
www.doodlebug.ws

Dove of the East
(888) 219-0382
www.doveoftheeast.com

Dream Street Papers
(480) 275-9736
www.dreamstreetpapers.com

Duncan Enterprises
(800) 438-6226
www.aleenes.com

Dymo
(800) 426-7827
www.dymo.com

EK Success, Ltd.
(800) 524-1349
www.eksuccess.com

Fancy Pants Designs, LLC
(801) 779-3212
www.fancypantsdesigns.com

Fiskars, Inc.
(866) 348-5661
www.fiskars.com

Flair Designs
(888) 546-9990
www.flairdesignsinc.com

FontWerks
(604) 942-3105
www.fontwerks.com

Frances Meyer, Inc.
(413) 584-5446
www.francesmeyer.com

Freckle Press — no contact info

Golden Artist Colors, Inc.
(800) 959-6543
www.goldenpaints.com

Grafix
(800) 447-2349
www.grafixarts.com

Hallmark Cards, Inc.
(800) 425-5627
www.hallmark.com

Hambly Screen Prints
(408) 496-1100
www.hamblyscreenprints.com

Heidi Grace Designs, Inc.
(866) 348-5661
www.heidigrace.com

Heidi Swapp/Advantus Corporation
(904) 482-0092
www.heidiswapp.com

Hero Arts Rubber Stamps, Inc.
(800) 822-4376
www.heroarts.com

Hobby Lobby Stores, Inc.
www.hobbylobby.com

Home Depot U.S.A., Inc.
www.homedepot.com

Hot Off The Press
(800) 227-9595
www.b2b.hotp.com

IBM
(800) 426-4968
www.ibm.com

Imagination Project, Inc.
(888) 477-6532
www.imaginationproject.com

Imaginisce
(801) 908-8111
www.imaginisce.com

JewelCraft, LLC
(201) 223-0804
www.jewelcraft.biz

Jo-Ann Stores
www.joann.com

JudiKins
(310) 515-1115
www.judikins.com

Junkitz
(732) 792-1108
www.junkitz.com

K&Company
(888) 244-2083
www.kandcompany.com

Karen Foster Design
(801) 451-9779
www.karenfosterdesign.com

KI Memories
(972) 243-5595
www.kimemories.com

Kodak
www.kodak.com

Krylon
(800) 457-9566
www.krylon.com

La Pluma, Inc.
(803) 749-4076
www.debrabeagle.com

Lasting Impressions for Paper, Inc.
(800) 936-2677
www.lastingimpressions.com

Leisure Arts/Memories in the Making
(800) 526-5111
www.leisurearts.com

Li'l Davis Designs
(480) 223-0080
www.lildavisdesigns.com

Little Black Dress Designs
(360) 897-8844
www.littleblackdressdesigns.com

Magic Mesh
(651) 345-6374
www.magicmesh.com

Magnetic Poetry
(800) 370-7697
www.magneticpoetry.com

Making Memories
(801) 294-0430
www.makingmemories.com

Marvy Uchida/Uchida of America, Corp.
(800) 541-5877
www.uchida.com

May Arts
(800) 442-3950
www.mayarts.com

Maya Road, LLC
(214) 488-3279
www.mayaroad.com

me & my BiG ideas
(949) 583-2065
www.meandmybigideas.com

Michaels Arts & Crafts
(800) 642-4235
www.michaels.com

Microsoft Corporation
www.microsoft.com

Miss Elizabeth's — no contact info

Mrs. Grossman's Paper Company
(800) 429-4549
www.mrsgrossmans.com

Mustard Moon
(763) 493-5157
www.mustardmoon.com

My Fonts
www.myfonts.com

My Mind's Eye, Inc.
(800) 665-5116
www.mymindseye.com

Office Max
www.officemax.com

Offray — see Berwick Offray, LLC

Old Time Pottery
www.oldtimepottery.com

One Heart...One Mind, LLC
(888) 414-3690

Paper Adventures — see ANW Crestwood

Paper Loft, The
(801) 254-1961
www.paperloft.com

Paper Salon
(800) 627-2648
www.papersalon.com

Paper Source
(888) 727-3711
www.paper-source.com

Paper Studio
(480) 557-5700
www.paperstudio.com

Pebbles Inc.
(801) 235-1520
www.pebblesinc.com

Per Annum, Inc.
(800) 548-1108
www.perannum.com

Petaloo
(800) 458-0350
www.petaloo.com

Pinecone Press
(714) 434-9881
www.pineconepressbooks.com

Plaid Enterprises, Inc.
(800) 842-4197
www.plaidonline.com

Posh Impressions
(800) 401-8644
www.poshimpressions.com

Pressed Petals
(800) 748-4656
www.pressedpetals.com

Prima Marketing, Inc.
(909) 627-5532
www.primamarketinginc.com

Provo Craft
(800) 937-7686
www.provocraft.com

PSX Design
www.sierra-enterprises.com/psxmain

Purple Onion Designs
www.purpleoniondesigns.com

Queen & Co.
(858) 613-7858
www.queenandcompany.com

QuicKutz, Inc.
(888) 702-1146
www.quickutz.com

Ranger Industries, Inc.
(800) 244-2211
www.rangerink.com

Reminisce Papers
(319) 358-9777
www.shopreminisce.com

Robin's Nest Press, The
(435) 789-5387
robins@sbnet.com

Rusty Pickle
(801) 746-1045
www.rustypickle.com

Scenic Route Paper Co.
(801) 225-5754
www.scenicroutepaper.com

Scrapsupply
(615) 777-3953
www.scrapsupply.com

Scraptivity Scrapbooking, Inc.
(800) 393-2151
www.scraptivity.com

Scrapworks, LLC/As You Wish Products, LLC
(801) 363-1010
www.scrapworks.com

SEI, Inc.
(800) 333-3279
www.shopsei.com

Shoebox Trims
(303) 257-7578
www.shoeboxtrims.com

Shrinky Dinks
(800) 445-7448
www.shrinkydinks.com

Sizzix
(877) 355-4766
www.sizzix.com

Stampendous!
(800) 869-0474
www.stampendous.com

Staples, Inc.
www.staples.com

Strano Designs
(508) 454-4615
www.stranodesigns.com

Stretch-Rite — no contact info

Sweetwater
(800) 359-3094
www.sweetwaterscrapbook.com

Swingline/ACCO Brands
(800) 820-6220
www.swingline.com

Target
www.target.com

Technique Tuesday, LLC
(503) 644-4073
www.techniquetuesday.com

Teters Floral Product
(800) 999-5996
www.teters.com

Therm O Web, Inc.
(800) 323-0799
www.thermoweb.com

Three Bugs in a Rug, LLC
(801) 804-6657
www.threebugsinarug.com

Tombow
(800) 835-3232
www.tombowusa.com

**Two Peas in a Bucket /
Kaboose Scrapbook, LLC**
(888) 896-7327
www.twopeasinabucket.com

Urban Lily
www.urbanlily.com

Wal-Mart Stores, Inc.
www.walmart.com

Watchfaces-Charms
(708) 352-3861
www.watchfaces-charms.com

We R Memory Keepers, Inc.
(801) 539-5000
www.weronthenet.com

Westrim Crafts
(800) 727-2727
www.westrimcrafts.com

Williams-Sonoma, Inc.
(877) 812-6235
www.williams-sonoma.com

Wishblade, Inc. — see Xyron

WorldWin Papers
(888) 834-6455
www.worldwinpapers.com

Wrights Ribbon Accents
(877) 597-4448
www.wrights.com

Wübie Prints
(888) 256-0107
www.wubieprints.com

Xyron
(800) 793-3523
www.xyron.com

Zsiage, LLC
(718) 224-1976
www.zsiage.com

index

Get more scrapbooking ideas from Memory Makers Masters!

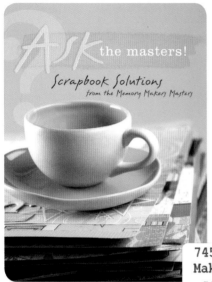

Ask The Masters!

Learn innovative techniques and
from the Memory Makers Master
creating flawless scrapbook page

ISBN-13: 978-1-892127-88-4
ISBN-10: 1-892127-88-1
paperback
128 pages
Z0277

...rtist Trudy Sigurdson
...themes from photographs
...g textiles, metals, natural
...paper and clear elements.

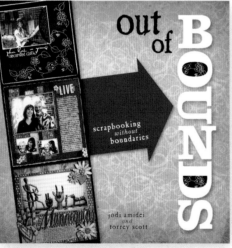

Out of Bounds

Push the boundaries of your scrapbooking
with creative inspiration and innovative
ideas from leading scrapbook designers
Jodi Amidei and Torrey Scott.

ISBN-13: 978-1-59963-009-0
ISBN-10: 1-59963-009-5
paperback
128 pages
Z0795

That's Life

Popular scrapbook designer Nic Howard
shows how to identify, capture and chronicle
everyday moments and daily routines in
endearing scrapbook pages.

ISBN-13: 978-1-59963-001-4
ISBN-10: 1-59963-001-X
paperback
112 pages
Z0689

These and other fine Memory Makers titles are available at your local scrapbook
or craft store, bookstore or from online suppliers, including *www.fwbookstore.com*.